Mastering AWS Security

Create and maintain a secure cloud ecosystem

Albert Anthony

BIRMINGHAM - MUMBAI

Mastering AWS Security

First published: October 2017

Production reference: 1251017

Published by Packt Publishing Ltd.
Livery Place
35 Livery Street
Birmingham
B3 2PB, UK.

ISBN 978-1-78829-372-3

www.packtpub.com

Credits

Author
Albert Anthony

Reviewers
Adrin Mukherjee
Satyajit Das

Commissioning Editor
Vijin Boricha

Acquisition Editor
Heramb Bhavsar

Content Development Editor
Devika Battike

Technical Editor
Prachi Sawant

Copy Editors
Juliana Nair
Stuti Srivastava

Project Coordinator
Judie Jose

Proofreader
Safis Editing

Indexer
Tejal Daruwale Soni

Graphics
Kirk D'Penha

Production Coordinator
Melwyn Dsa

About the Author

Albert Anthony is a seasoned IT professional with 18 years of experience working with various technologies and in multiple teams spread all across the globe. He believes that the primary purpose of information technology is to solve problems faced by businesses and organizations. He is an AWS certified solutions architect and a corporate trainer. He holds all three AWS associate-level certifications along with PMI-PMP and Certified Scrum Master certifications. He has been training since 2008 on project management, cost management, and people management, and on AWS since 2016.

He has managed multiple projects on AWS that runs big data applications, hybrid mobile application development, DevOps, and infrastructure monitoring on AWS. He has successfully migrated multiple workloads to AWS from on-premise data centers and other hosting providers. He is responsible for securing workloads for all his customers, with hundreds of servers; processing TBs of data; and running multiple web, mobile, and batch applications. As well as this, he and his team has saved their customers millions of dollars by optimizing usage of their AWS resources and following AWS best practices.

Albert has worked with organizations of all shapes and sizes in India, the USA, and the Middle East. He has worked with government organizations, non-profit organizations, banks and financial institutions, and others to deliver transformational projects. He has worked as a programmer, system analyst, project manager, and senior engineering manager throughout his career. He is the founder of a cloud training and consulting startup, LovesCloud, in New Delhi, India.

I want to thank the staff at Packt Publishing, namely Heramb, Devika, and Prachi, for giving me the opportunity to author this book and helping me over the past few months to bring this book to life.

About the Reviewers

Adrin Mukherjee, solution architect for Wipro Limited, is a core member of the engineering team that drives Wipro's Connected Cars Platform. He has thirteen years of IT experience and has had several challenging roles as a technical architect, building distributed applications, and high performance systems.

He loves to spend his personal time with his family and his best friend Choco, a Labrador Retriever.

Satyajit Das has more than seventeen years of industry experience including around four years of experience in AWS and Google cloud. He helped internal and external customers for defining architecture of applications to be hosted in cloud. He has defined migration factory and led teams for application migration. He has used Enterprise architecture framework to define application, data and infrastructure architecture and migrate solutions to AWS cloud. He architected, designed and implemented high available, scalable and fault tolerant applications using Micro-Service architecture paradigm and used cloud native architecture in AWS. He has also been involved with cloud CoE, governance setup, defining best practices, policies and guidelines for service implementations. He has lead large teams for solution delivery and execution. He has experience across industry domains like manufacturing, finance, consulting, and government.

Satyajit has worked in leading organizations such as Wipro, Infosys, PwC and Accenture in various challenging roles.

Satyajit has co-authored AWS Networking Cookbook

> *I'll like to thank my entire family specially my wife Papiya for supporting me in all ups and downs.*

www.PacktPub.com

For support files and downloads related to your book, please visit www.PacktPub.com.

Did you know that Packt offers eBook versions of every book published, with PDF and ePub files available? You can upgrade to the eBook version at www.PacktPub.com and as a print book customer, you are entitled to a discount on the eBook copy. Get in touch with us at service@packtpub.com for more details.

At www.PacktPub.com, you can also read a collection of free technical articles, sign up for a range of free newsletters and receive exclusive discounts and offers on Packt books and eBooks.

https://www.packtpub.com/mapt

Get the most in-demand software skills with Mapt. Mapt gives you full access to all Packt books and video courses, as well as industry-leading tools to help you plan your personal development and advance your career.

why subscribe

- Fully searchable across every book published by Packt
- Copy and paste, print, and bookmark content
- On demand and accessible via a web browser

Customer Feedback

Thanks for purchasing this Packt book. At Packt, quality is at the heart of our editorial process. To help us improve, please leave us an honest review on this book's Amazon page at `https://www.amazon.com/dp/178829372X`.

If you'd like to join our team of regular reviewers, you can e-mail us at `customerreviews@packtpub.com`. We award our regular reviewers with free eBooks and videos in exchange for their valuable feedback. Help us be relentless in improving our products!

Table of Contents

Preface

Security in information technology is considered a nerdy or geeky topic, reserved for technologists who know about the nitty-gritty of networks, packets, algorithms, and so on for years. With organizations moving their workloads, applications, and infrastructure to the cloud at an unprecedented pace, security of all these resources has been a paradigm shift for all those who are responsible for security; experts, novices, and apprentices alike. AWS provides many controls to secure customer workloads and quite often customers are not aware of their share of security responsibilities, and the security controls that they need to own and put in place for their resources in the AWS cloud. This book aims to resolve this problem by providing detailed information, in easy-to-understand language, supported by real-life examples, figures, and screenshots, for all you need to know about security in AWS, without being a geek or a nerd and without having years of experience in the security domain!

This book tells you how you can enable continuous security, continuous auditing, and continuous compliance by automating your security in AWS; with tools, services, and features provided by AWS. By the end of this book, you will understand the complete landscape of security in AWS, covering all aspects of end-to-end software and hardware security along with logging, auditing, and the compliance of your entire IT environment in the AWS cloud. Use the best practices mentioned in this book to master security in your AWS environment.

What this book covers

Chapter 1, *Overview of Security in AWS*, introduces you to the shared security responsibility model, a fundamental concept to understand security in AWS. As well as this, it introduces you to the security landscape in AWS.

Chapter 2, *AWS Identity and Access Management*, walks you through the doorway of all things about security in AWS, access control, and user management. We learn about identities and authorizations for everything in AWS in great detail in this chapter.

Chapter 3, *AWS Virtual Private Cloud*, talks about creating and securing our own virtual network in the AWS cloud. This chapter also introduces you to the various connectivity options that AWS provides to create hybrid cloud, public cloud, and private cloud solutions.

Chapter 4, *Data Security in AWS*, talks about encryption in AWS to secure your data in rest and while working with AWS data storage services.

Chapter 5, *Securing Servers in AWS*, explains ways to secure your infrastructure in AWS by employing continuous threat assessment, agent-based security checks, virtual firewalls for your servers, and so on.

Chapter 6, *Securing Applications in AWS*, introduces you to ways to secure all your applications developed and deployed in the AWS environment. This chapter walks you through the web application firewall service, as well as securing a couple of AWS services used by developers for web and mobile application development.

Chapter 7, *Monitoring in AWS*, provides a deep dive into the monitoring of your resources in AWS, including AWS services, resources, and applications running on the AWS cloud. This chapter helps you to set up monitoring for your native AWS resources along with your custom applications and resources.

Chapter 8, *Logging and Auditing in AWS*, helps you to learn ways to stay compliant in the AWS cloud by logging and auditing all that is going on with your AWS resources. This chapter gives you a comprehensive, hands-on tour of logging and auditing all the services to achieve continuous compliance for your AWS environment.

Chapter 9, *AWS Security Best Practices*, walks you through best practices in a consolidated form for securing all your resources in AWS. Ensure that these best practices are followed for all your AWS environments!

What you need for this book

You will need to sign up for the AWS Free Tier account available at https://aws.amazon. com/free/ for this book. That is all you need, an AWS Free Tier account and the basic understanding of AWS foundation services, such as AWS Simple Storage Service, Amazon Elastic Compute Cloud, and so on.

Who this book is for

This book is for all IT professionals, system administrators, security analysts, and chief information security officers who are responsible for securing workloads in AWS for their organizations. It is helpful for all solutions architects who want to design and implement secure architecture on AWS by following the security by design principle. This book is helpful for people in auditing and project management roles to understand how they can audit AWS workloads and how they can manage security in AWS respectively.

If you are learning AWS or championing AWS adoption in your organization, you should read this book to build security into all your workloads. You will benefit from knowing about the security footprint of all major AWS services for multiple domains, use cases, and scenarios.

Conventions

In this book, you will find a number of styles of text that distinguish between different kinds of information. Here are some examples of these styles, and an explanation of their meaning.

Code words in text, database table names, folder names, filenames, file extensions, pathnames, dummy URLs, user input, and Twitter handles are shown as follows: "Amazon EC2 key pair that is stored within AWS is appended to the initial operating system user's `~/.ssh/authorized_keys` file".

A block of code is as follows:

```
{
  "Version": "2012-10-17",
  "Statement": [
  {
  "Effect": "Allow",
  "Action": "ec2:Describe*",
  "Resource": "*"
  }
  ]
  }
```

New terms and important words are shown in bold. Words that you see on the screen, in menus or dialog boxes for example, appear in the text like this: "Statistic chosen is **Average** and the period is **5 Minutes**:"

Warnings or important notes appear like this

Tips and tricks appear like this.

Readers feedback

Feedback from our readers is always welcome. Let us know what you think about this book-what you liked or disliked. Reader feedback is important for us as it helps us develop titles that you will really get the most out of.

To send us general feedback, simply email `feedback@packtpub.com`, and mention the book's title in the subject of your message.

If there is a topic that you have expertise in and you are interested in either writing or contributing to a book, see our author guide at `www.packtpub.com/authors`.

Customer support

Now that you are the proud owner of a Packt book, we have a number of things to help you to get the most from your purchase.

Downloading the color images of this book

We also provide you with a PDF file that has color images of the screenshots/diagrams used in this book. The color images will help you better understand the changes in the output. You can download this file from `https://www.packtpub.com/sites/default/files/downloads/MasteringAWSSecurity_ColorImages.pdf`.

Errata

Although we have taken every care to ensure the accuracy of our content, mistakes do happen. If you find a mistake in one of our books-maybe a mistake in the text or the code-we would be grateful if you could report this to us. By doing so, you can save other readers from frustration and help us improve subsequent versions of this book. If you find any errata, please report them by visiting `http://www.packtpub.com/submit-errata`, selecting your book, clicking on the **Errata Submission Form** link, and entering the details of your errata. Once your errata are verified, your submission will be accepted and the errata will be uploaded to our website or added to any list of existing errata under the Errata section of that title.

To view the previously submitted errata, go to `https://www.packtpub.com/books/content/support` and enter the name of the book in the search field. The required information will appear under the **Errata** section.

Piracy

Piracy of copyrighted material on the Internet is an ongoing problem across all media. At Packt, we take the protection of our copyright and licenses very seriously. If you come across any illegal copies of our works in any form on the Internet, please provide us with the location address or website name immediately so that we can pursue a remedy.

Please contact us at copyright@packtpub.com with a link to the suspected pirated material.

We appreciate your help in protecting our authors and our ability to bring you valuable content.

Questions

If you have a problem with any aspect of this book, you can contact us at questions@packtpub.com, and we will do our best to address the problem.

1
Overview of Security in AWS

AWS provides many services, tools and methods such as access control, firewall, encryption, logging, monitoring, compliance, and so on to secure your journey in cloud. These AWS services supports plethora of use cases and scenarios to take end to end care of all your security, logging, auditing and compliance requirement in cloud environment. There is AWS **Identity and Access Management (IAM)** service that allows you to control access and actions for your AWS users and resources securely, **Virtual Private Cloud (VPC)** allows you to secure your infrastructure in AWS cloud by creating a virtual network similar to your own private network in your on premises data center.

Moreover, there are web services such as **Key Management Services (KMS)** that facilitates key management and encryption for protecting your data at rest and in transit. There is AWS Shield and AWS **Web Application Firewall (WAF)** to protect your AWS resources and applications from common security threats such as **Distributed Denial of Service (DDoS)** by configuring firewalls at various levels.

AWS Config along with AWS CloudTrail and AWS CloudWatch supports logging, auditing and configuration management for all your AWS resources. AWS Artifact is a managed self-service that gives you compliance documents on demand for all your compliance requirements from your auditor.

This book aims to explain the preceding mentioned services, tools, and methods to enable you in automating all security controls using services provided by AWS such as AWS Lambda, AWS **Simple Notification Service (SNS)**, and so on. We will learn how compliance is different from security. We will learn about how security can be implemented as a continuous activity instead of a periodic activity and how we can achieve continuous compliance by using AWS services. This chapter will give you an overview of security in **Amazon Web Services**, popularly known as AWS or AWS cloud. We'll learn about the shared security responsibility model of AWS that lies at the very foundation of AWS Security.

Chapter overview

In this chapter, we will learn about security in AWS cloud. We will learn about security processes in place to secure all workloads deployed in AWS environment. We will begin by exploring AWS shared security responsibility model, a primer for all thing security in AWS. To secure anything, we first need to know who is responsible for security. We will deep dive into this fundamental principle of AWS Security to know about security responsibilities of AWS and users of AWS services for various models that AWS offers to all its customers.

Moving on, we will go through AWS Security responsibilities in detail across multiple verticals such as physical security, network security, and so on. We will also go through various processes AWS has put in place to ensure business continuity and seamless communication in event of an incident. Alongside, we will walk through customer security responsibilities for all workloads deployed in AWS cloud. This will include things such as protecting credentials, data security, access control, and so on.

Furthermore, we will go through security features of your AWS account.

Next, we will go through overview of all security services and features provided by AWS such as KMS, CloudWatch, Shield, CloudTrail, penetration testing, and so on.

Lastly, we will go through various resources available in AWS for learning more about these security services and features. These resources include AWS documentation, white papers, blogs, tutorials, solutions, and so on.

AWS shared security responsibility model

AWS and cloud in general have evolved considerably from the time when security in cloud was seen as an impediment to moving your data, applications, and workload to cloud to today when security in cloud is one of the major reasons organizations are moving from data centers to cloud. More and more executives, decision makers, and key stakeholders are vouching that security in cloud is further ahead, and more reliable and economical than security in on-premise data centers. These executives and decision makers are from multiple geographies, and various industries with stringent security requirements and regulatory compliance such as Department of Defense, Banking, Health Care, Payment Card Industry, and so on, and belong to all levels such as CIO, CTO, CEO, CISO, System Administrators, Project Managers, Developers, Security Analysts, and so on.

As a result, cloud adoption rate has been rapidly increasing for the past few years across the globe and across industries. This trend is led by large enterprises where security plays a pivotal role in deciding if an enterprise should move to the cloud or not. AWS provides fully integrated and unified security solutions for its cloud services that enables its customers to migrate their workloads to cloud. Let us look at some predictions for the exponential growth of Cloud Computing by industry leaders:

- Gartner says that by 2020, a corporate no-cloud policy will be as rare as the no-internet policy today.
- **Global Cloud Index (GCI)** forecasts that cloud will account for 92% of the data center by 2020, meaning 92% of all data and computing resources will be using cloud by 2020.
- **International Data Corporation (IDC)** says that today's cloud first strategy is already moving the towards cloud.

AWS is architected to be one of the most flexible and secure cloud environments. It removes most of the security burdens that are traditionally associated with IT infrastructure. AWS ensures complete customer privacy and segregation of customer resources and has scores of built-in security features. Moreover, every customer benefits from the security processes, global infrastructure and network architecture put in place by AWS to comply with stringent security and compliance requirements by thousands of customers across the globe from scores of industries.

As more and more organizations move towards cloud, security in cloud has been more of a paradigm shift for many. Even though for the most part, security that is provided in cloud has most of the same functionalities as security in traditional IT, such as protecting information from theft, data leakage, and deletion.

However, security in the cloud is in fact slightly different to security in an on-premises data center. When you move servers, data and workload to AWS cloud, responsibilities are shared between you and AWS for securing your data and workload. AWS is responsible for securing the underlying infrastructure that supports the cloud through its global network of regions, availability zones, edge locations, end points, and so on, and customers are responsible for anything they put on the cloud such as their data, their application, or anything that they connect to the cloud such as the servers in their data centers. They are also responsible for providing access to their virtual network and resources in cloud, this model is known as **AWS shared security responsibility model**.

The following figure depicts this model:

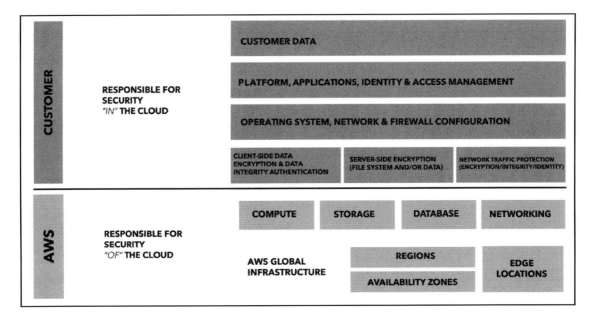

Figure 1 - AWS shared security responsibility model

In order to master AWS Security, it is imperative for us to identify and understand AWS' share of security responsibilities as well as our share of security responsibilities before we start implementing them. AWS offers a host of different services that can be distributed in three broad categories: infrastructure, container, and abstracted services. Each of these categories has its own security ownership model based on how end users interact with it and how the functionality is accessed:

- **Infrastructure Services**: This category includes compute services such as Amazon **Elastic Cloud Compute (EC2)** and associated services, such as Amazon **Elastic Block Store (EBS)**, Elastic Load Balancing, and Amazon **Virtual Private Cloud (VPC)**. These services let you design and build your own secure and private network on cloud with infrastructure similar to your on-premises solutions. This network in AWS cloud is also compatible and can be integrated with your on-premises network. You control the operating system, configure the firewall rules and operate any identity management system that provides access to the user layer of the virtualization stack.

- **Container Services**: There are certain AWS services that run on separate Amazon EC2 or other infrastructure instances but at times you don't manage the operating system or the platform layer. AWS offers these services in a managed services model for these application containers. You are responsible for configuring firewall rules, allowing access to your users and systems for these services using AWS **Identity and Access Management (IAM)** among other things. These services include AWS Elastic Beanstalk, Amazon **Elastic Map Reduce (EMR)** and Amazon **Relational Database Services (RDS)**.

- **Abstracted Services**: These are AWS services that abstract the platform or management layer. These are messaging, email, NoSQL database, and storage services on which you can build and operate cloud applications. These services are accessed through endpoints by using AWS APIs. AWS manages the underlying service components or the operating system on which they reside. You share the underlying infrastructure that AWS provides for these abstracted services. These services provide a multi-tenant platform which isolates your data from other users. These services are integrated with AWS IAM for secure access and usage. These services include Simple Queue Service, Amazon DynamoDB, SNS, Amazon **Simple Storage Service (S3)**, and so on.

Let us look at these 3 categories in detail along with their shared security responsibility models:

Shared responsibility model for infrastructure services

AWS global infrastructure powers AWS infrastructure services such as Amazon EC2, Amazon VPC and Amazon **Elastic Block Storage (EBS)**. These are regional services; that is, they operate within the region where they have been launched. They have different durability and availability objectives. However, it is possible to build systems exceeding availability objectives of individual services from AWS. AWS provides multiple options to use various resilient components in multiple availability zones inside a region to design highly available systems.

The following figure shows this model:

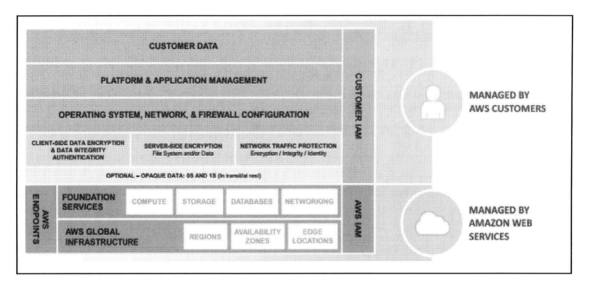

Figure 2 - Shared responsibility model for infrastructure services

Building on the AWS secure global infrastructure, similar to your on-premises data centers, you will install, configure, and manage your operating systems and platforms in the AWS cloud. Once you have your platform, you will use it to install your applications and then you will store your data on that platform. You will configure the security of your data such as encryption in transit and at rest. You are responsible for managing how your applications and end users consume this data. If your business requires more layers of protection due to compliance or other regulatory requirements, you can always add it on top of those provided by AWS global infrastructure security layers.

These layers of protection might include securing data at rest by using encryption, or securing data in transit or by introducing additional layer of opacity between AWS services and your platform. This layer could includes secure time stamping, temporary security credentials, data encryption, software and passing digital signature in your API requests and so on.

AWS provides tools and technologies that can be used to protect your data at rest and in transit. We'll take a detailed look at these technologies in `Chapter 4`, *Data Security in AWS*.

When you launch a new Amazon **Elastic Cloud Compute (EC2)** instance from a standard **Amazon Machine Image (AMI)**, you can access it using the secure remote system access protocols, such as **Secure Shell (SSH)** for a Linux instance or Windows **Remote Desktop Protocol (RDP)** for a Windows instance. To configure your EC2 instance as per your requirements and to access it, you are required to authenticate at the operating-system level. Once you have authenticated at the operating system level, you'll have secure remote access to the Amazon EC2 instance. You can then set up multiple methods to authenticate operating systems such as Microsoft Active Directory, X.509 certificate authentication, or local operating system accounts.

AWS provides Amazon EC2 key pairs that consist of two different keys, a public key and a private key. These RSA key pairs are the industry standard and used for authentication to access your EC2 instance. When you launch a new EC2 instance, you get an option to either create a new key pair or use an existing key pair. There is a third option available as well to proceed without a key pair, but that is not recommended for securing access to your EC2 instance. The following figure 3 shows the EC2 key pairs option while launching an EC2 instance. You can create as many as 5000 key pairs for your EC2 instances in your AWS account. EC2 key pairs are used only for accessing your EC2 instances and cannot be used to login to AWS Management Console or to use other AWS services. Moreover, users can use different key pairs to access different EC2 instances:

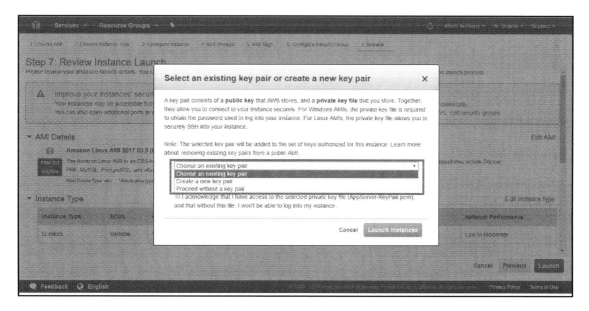

Figure 3 - AWS key pairs

You can either have AWS generate the EC2 key pairs for you, or you can generate your own Amazon EC2 key pairs using industry standard tools like OpenSSL. When you choose the first option, AWS provides you with both the public and private key of the RSA key pair when you launch the instance. You need to securely store the private key; if it is lost you can't restore it from AWS, and you will then have to generate a new key pair.

When you launch a new Linux EC2 instance using a standard AWS AMI, the public key of the Amazon EC2 key pair that is stored within AWS is appended to the initial operating system user's `~/.ssh/authorized_keys` file. You can use an SSH client to connect to this EC2 Linux instance by configuring the SSH client to use the EC2's username such as `ec2-user` and by using the private key for authorizing a user.

When you launch a new Windows EC2 instance using the `ec2config` service from a standard AWS AMI, the `ec2config` service sets a new random administrator password for this Windows instance and encrypts it using the corresponding Amazon EC2 key pair's public key. You will use the private key to decrypt the default administrator's password. This password will be used for user authentication on the Windows instance.

Although AWS provides plenty of flexible and practical tools for managing Amazon EC2 keys and authentication for accessing EC2 instances, if you require higher security due to your business requirements or regulatory compliance, you can always implement other authentication mechanisms such as **Lightweight Directory Access Protocol** (**LDAP**) and disable the Amazon EC2 key pair authentication.

Shared responsibility model for container services

The AWS shared responsibility model is applicable to container services as well, such as Amazon EMR and Amazon RDS. For these services, AWS manages the operating system, underlying infrastructure, application platform, and foundation services. For example, Amazon RDS for Microsoft SQL server is a managed database service where AWS manages all the layers of the container including the Microsoft SQL server database platform. Even though AWS platform provides data backup and recovery tools for services such as Amazon RDS, it is your responsibility to plan, configure and use tools to prepare for your **high availability (HA)**, **fault tolerance (FT)**, **business continuity and disaster recovery (BCDR)** strategy.

You are responsible for securing your data, for providing access to your data and for configuring firewall rules to access these container services. Examples of firewall rules include RDS security groups for Amazon RDS and EC2 security groups for Amazon EMR.

The following figure shows this model for container services:

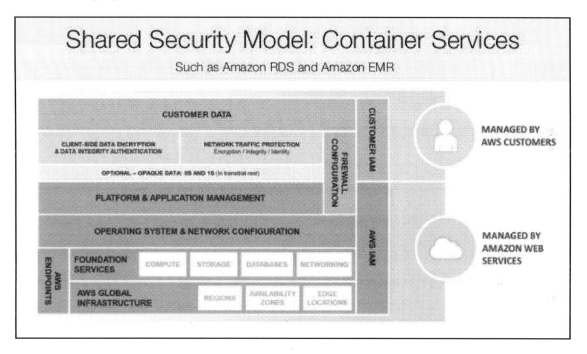

Figure 4 - Shared responsibility model for container services

Shared responsibility model for abstracted services

AWS offers abstracted services such as Amazon DynamoDB and Amazon Simple Queue Service, Amazon S3, and so on, where you can access endpoints of these services for storing, modifying and retrieving data. AWS is responsible for managing these services, that is, operating the infrastructure layer, installing and updating the operating system and managing platforms as well. These services are tightly integrated with IAM so you can decide who can access your data stored in these services.

You are also responsible for classifying your data and using service-specific tools for configuring permissions at the platform level for individual resources. By using IAM, you can also configure permissions based on role, user identity or user groups. Amazon S3 provides you with encryption of data at rest at the platform level, and, for data in transit, it provides HTTPS encapsulation through signing API requests.

The following figure shows this model for abstracted services:

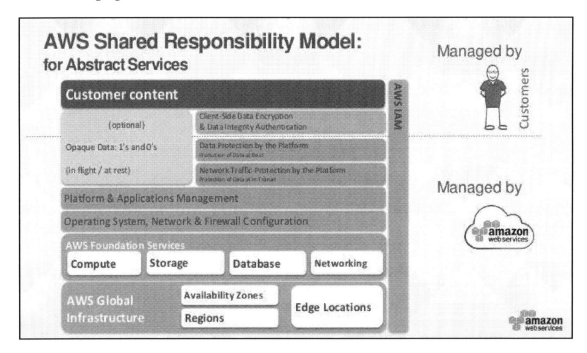

Figure 5 - Shared responsibility model for abstracted services

AWS Security responsibilities

AWS is responsible for securing the global infrastructure that includes regions, availability zones and edge locations running on the AWS cloud. These availability zones host multiple data centers that house hardware, software, networking, and other resources that run AWS services. Securing this infrastructure is AWS's number one priority and AWS is regularly audited by reputed agencies all over the world to meet necessary security and compliance standard requirements. These audit reports are available to customers from AWS as customers can't visit AWS data centers in person.

The following figure depicts the broader areas of security that fall under AWS' responsibility:

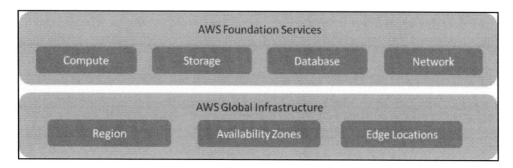

Figure 6 - AWS shared security model - AWS responsibilities

Customer data and workloads are stored in AWS data centers, these data centers are spread across geographical regions all over world. These data centers are owned, operated and controlled by AWS. This control includes physical access and entry to these data centers and all networking components and hardware, and all other additional data centers that are part of AWS global infrastructure.

Let us take a closer look at other responsibilities that AWS owns for securing its global infrastructure:

Physical and environmental security

So, the very first thought that would strike anybody considering moving their workload to cloud is where is my data actually stored? Where are those physical servers and hard drives located that I provisioned using AWS cloud? And how are those hardware resources secured and who secures them? After all cloud simply virtualizes all resources available in a data center but those resources are present somewhere physically. So, the good news is AWS is completely responsible for physical and environmental security of all hardware resources located in its data centers across the globe.

AWS has years of experience in building, managing, and securing large data centers across the globe through its parent company Amazon. AWS ensures that all of its data centers are secured using the best technology and processes such as housing them in nondescript facilities, following least privilege policy, video surveillance, two-factor authentication for entering data centers and floors.

Personnel are not allowed on data center floors unless they have a requirement to access a physical data storage device in person. Moreover, AWS firmly implements segregation of responsibilities principle, so any personnel having access to the physical device won't have the root user access for that device so he can't access data on that physical device.

This is a very critical part of a shared security responsibility model where AWS does all the heavy lifting instead of you worrying about the physical and environmental security of your data centers. You do not have to worry about monitoring, theft, intrusion, fire, natural calamities, power failure, and so on for your data centers. These things are taken care of by AWS on your behalf and they constantly upgrade their security procedures to keep up with increasing threats.

Storage device decommissioning

AWS will initiate a decommissioning process when a storage device has reached the end of its useful life. This process ensures that customer data is not exposed to unauthorized individuals. This hardware device will be physically destroyed or degaussed if it fails decommissioning using the standard process followed by AWS.

Business continuity management

AWS keeps your data and other resources in the data centers in various geographical locations across the globe; these locations are known as regions. Each region has two or more availability zones for high availability and fault tolerance. These availability zones are made up of one or more data centers. All of these data centers are in use and none are kept offline; that is, there aren't any cold data centers. These data centers house all the physical hardware resources such as servers, storage, and networking devices, and so on, that are required to keep all the AWS services up and running as per the service level agreement provided by AWS. All AWS core applications such as compute, storage, databases, networking are deployed in an N+1 configuration, so that, in the event of a data center failure due to natural calamity, human error or any other unforeseen circumstance, there is sufficient capacity to load-balance traffic to the remaining sites.

Each availability zone is designed as an independent failure zone so that the impact of failure is minimum and failure can be contained by other availability zone(s) in that region. They are physically separated within a geographical location and are situated in the lower risk flood plains.

Depending on the nature of your business, regulatory compliance, performance requirements, disaster recovery, fault tolerance, and so on, you might decide to design your applications to be distributed across multiple regions so that they are available even if a region is unavailable.

The following figure demonstrates typical regions with their availability zones:

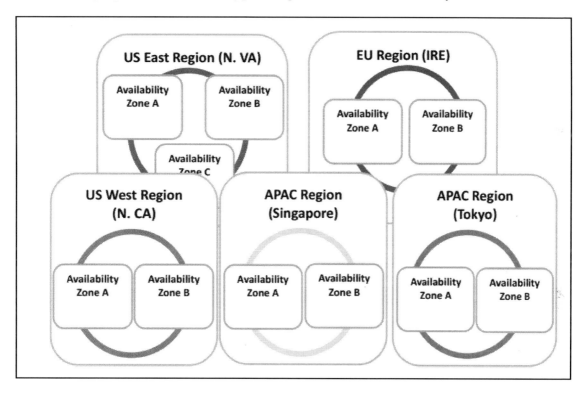

Figure 7 - AWS regions and availability zones

Communication

AWS employs multiple methods of external and internal communication to keep their customers and global AWS communities updated about all the necessary security events that might impact any AWS service. There are several processes in place to notify the customer support team about operational issues impacting customer experience globally, regionally or for a particular AWS service. AWS provides a Service Health Dashboard at https://status.aws.amazon.com that provides updates about all AWS services.

It also has an option to notify AWS about any issue customers are facing with any AWS service. The AWS Security center is available to provide you with security and compliance details about AWS. There are 4 support plans available at AWS:

- Basic
- Developer
- Business
- Enterprise

These support plans give you various levels of interaction capabilities with AWS support teams such as AWS technical support, health status and notifications, and so on. However, 24/7 access to customer service and communities is available to all AWS customers irrespective of the support plan subscription.

The following figure shows the AWS Service Health Dashboard for all North America, you can also get information for service health in other geographies such as Asia Pacific, Europe, and so on:

Figure 8 - AWS Service Health Dashboard

Network security

The AWS network has been architected to allow you to configure the appropriate levels of security for your business, your workload, and your regulatory compliance requirements. It enables you to build geographically dispersed, highly available, and fault-tolerant web architectures with a host of cloud resources that are managed and monitored by AWS.

Secure network architecture

AWS has network devices such as a firewall to monitor and control communications at the external and key internal boundaries of the network. These network devices use configurations, **access control lists** (**ACL**) and rule sets to enforce the flow of information to specific information system services. Traffic flow policies or ACLs are established on each managed interface that enforces and manage traffic flow. These policies are approved by Amazon information security. An ACL management tool is used to automatically push these policies, to help ensure these managed interfaces enforce the most up-to-date ACLs.

Secure access points

AWS monitors network traffic and inbound and outbound communications through strategically placed access points in the cloud; these access points are also known as API endpoints. They allow secure HTTP access (HTTPS) through API signing process in AWS, allowing you to establish a secure communication session with your compute instances or storage resources within AWS.

Transmission protection

You can connect to an AWS access point through HTTP or HTTPS using **Secure Sockets Layer** (**SSL**). AWS provides customers with VPC, their own virtual network in cloud dedicated to the customer's AWS account. VPC is helpful for customers who require additional layers of network security. VPC allows communication with customer data centers through an encrypted tunnel using an IPsec **Virtual Private Network** (**VPN**) device.

Network monitoring and protection

AWS ensures a high level of service performance and availability by employing multiple automated monitoring systems. These tools monitor unauthorized intrusion attempts, server and network usage, application usage, and port scanning activities. AWS monitoring tools watch over ingress and egress communication points to detect conditions and unusual or unauthorized activities. Alarms go off automatically when thresholds are breached on key operational metrics to notify operations and management personnel. To handle any operational issues, AWS has trained call leaders to facilitate communication and progress during such events collaboratively. AWS convenes post operational issues that are significant in nature, irrespective of external impact, and **Cause of Error** (COE) documents are created so that preventive actions are taken in future, based on the root cause of the issue.

AWS access

The AWS production network is logically segregated from the Amazon corporate network and requires a separate set of credentials. It uses a complex set of network segregation and security devices for isolating these two networks. All AWS developers and administrators who need to access AWS cloud components for maintenance are required to raise a ticket for accessing AWS production network. In order to access the production network, Kerberos, user IDs, and passwords are required by Amazon corporate network. The AWS production network uses a different protocol; this network mandates the usage of SSH public-key authentication through a computer in a public domain often known as bastion host or jump box for AWS developers and administrators.

Credentials policy

AWS Security has established a credentials policy with the required configurations and expiration intervals. Passwords are regularly rotated once every 90 days and they are required to be complex.

Customer security responsibilities

AWS shares security responsibilities with customers for all its offerings. Essentially, the customer is responsible for security of everything that they decide to put in cloud such as data, applications, resources, and so on. So network protection and instance protection for IaaS services and database protection for container services are areas that fall under customer security responsibilities. Let us look at customer security responsibilities for these three categories:

For AWS infrastructure services, the customer is responsible for the following:

- Customer data
- Customer application
- Operating system
- Network and firewall configuration
- Customer identity and access management
- Instance management
- Data protection (transit, rest, and backup)
- Ensuring high availability and auto scaling resources

For AWS container services, the customer is responsible for the following:

- Customer data
- Network VPC and firewall configuration
- Customer identity and access management (DB users and table permissions)
- Ensuring high availability
- Data protection (transit, rest, and backup)
- Auto scaling resources

For AWS abstract services, the customer is responsible for the following:

- Customer data
- Securing data at rest using your own encryption
- Customer identity and access management

So essentially when we move from AWS infrastructure services towards AWS abstract services, customer security responsibility is limited to configuration, and operational security is handled by AWS. Moreover, AWS infrastructure services gives you many more options to integrate with on-premises security tools than AWS abstract services.

 All AWS products that are offered as IaaS such as Amazon EC2, Amazon S3, and Amazon VPC are completely under customer control. These services require the customer to configure security parameters for accessing these resources and performing management tasks. For example, for EC2 instances, the customer is responsible for management of the guest operating system including updates and security patches, installation and maintenance of any application software or utilities on the instances, and security group (firewall at the instance level, provided by AWS) configuration for each instance. These are essentially the same security tasks that the customer performs no matter where their servers are located. The following figure depicts customer responsibilities for the AWS shared security responsibilities model:

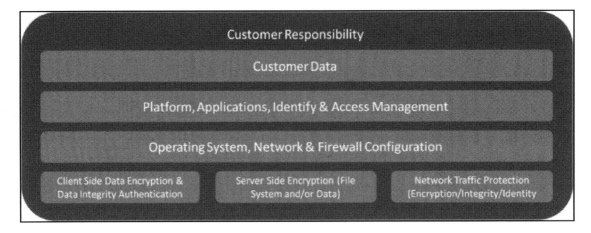

Figure 9 AWS shared security model - customer responsibilities

AWS provides a plethora of security services and tools to secure practically any workloads, but the customer has to actually implement the necessary defenses using those security services and tools.

At the top of the stack lies customer data. AWS recommends that you utilize appropriate safeguards such as encryption to protect data in transit and at rest. Safeguards also include fine-grained access controls to objects, creating and controlling the encryption keys used to encrypt your data, selecting appropriate encryption or tokenization methods, integrity validation, and appropriate retention of data. Customer chooses where to place their data in cloud, meaning they choose geographical location to store their data in cloud. In AWS, this geographical location is known as region, so customer has to choose an AWS region to store their data. Customers are also responsible for securing access to this data. Data is neither replicated to another AWS Region nor moved to other AWS Region unless customer decides to do it. Essentially, customers always own their data and they have full control over encrypting it, storing it at a desired geographical location, moving it to another geographical location or deleting it.

For AWS container services such as Amazon RDS, the customer doesn't need to worry about managing the infrastructure, patch update or installation of any application software. The customer is responsible for securing access to these services using Amazon IAM. The customer is also responsible for enabling **Multi-Factor Authentication (MFA)** for securing their AWS account access.

As a customer, you get to decide on security controls that you want to put in place based on the sensitivity of your data and applications. You have complete ownership of your data. You get to choose from a host of tools and services available across networking, encryption, identity and access management, and compliance.

The following table shows a high-level classification of security responsibilities for AWS and the customer:

AWS	Customer
Facility operations	Choice of guest operating system
Physical security	Configuring application options
Physical infrastructure	AWS account management
Network infrastructure	Configuring security groups (firewall)
Virtualization infrastructure	ACL
Hardware lifecycle management	IAM

Table 2 - AWS Security responsibilities classification

AWS account security features

Now that we are clear with the shared security responsibilities model, let us deep dive into the resources provided by AWS to secure your AWS account and resources inside your AWS account from unauthorized use. AWS gives you a host of tools for securing your account such as MFA, several options for credentials that can be used to access AWS services and accounts for multiple use cases, secure endpoints to communicate with AWS services, centralized logging service for collecting, storing and analyzing logs generated for all user activities in your AWS account by your resources in your AWS account and logs from all your applications running in your AWS account. Along with these features, you also have AWS Trusted Advisor that performs security checks for all AWS services in your AWS account. All of these tools are generic in nature and they are not tied to any specific service; they can be used with multiple services.

AWS account

This is the account that you create when you first sign up for AWS. It is also known as a **root account** in AWS terminology. This root account has a username as your email address and password that you use with this username. These credentials are used to log into your AWS account through the AWS Management Console, a web application to manage your AWS resources. This root account has administrator access for all AWS services, hence AWS does not recommend using root account credentials for day-to-day interactions with AWS; instead, they recommend creating another user with the required privileges to perform those activities. In some cases, your organization might decide to use multiple AWS accounts, one for each department or entity for example, and then create IAM users within each of the AWS accounts for the appropriate people and resources.

Let us look at the following scenarios for choosing strategies for AWS account creation:

Business requirement	Proposed design	Comments
Centralized security management	One AWS account	Centralizes information security management and minimal overhead.
Separation of production, development, and testing environments	Three AWS accounts	One account each for production, development, and the testing environment.

Multiple autonomous departments	Multiple AWS accounts	One account each for every autonomous department of organization. Assigns access control and permissions for every single account. Benefits from economies of scale.
Centralized security management with multiple autonomous independent projects	Multiple AWS accounts	Creates one AWS account for shared project resources such as Domain Name Service, User Database, and so on. Create one AWS account for each autonomous independent project and grant them permissions at granular level.

Table 3 - AWS account strategies

Having multiple AWS accounts also helps in decreasing your blast radius and reducing your disaster recovery time. So if there is something wrong with one AWS account, the impact will be minimal on running business operations, as other accounts will be working as usual along with their resources. Having multiple AWS accounts also increases security by segregating your resources across accounts based on the principle of least privilege.

AWS credentials

AWS uses several types of credentials for authentication and authorization as follows:

- Passwords
- Multi-factor authentication
- Access keys
- Key pairs
- X.509 certificates

We will have a detailed look at these credentials in Chapter 2, *AWS Identity and Access Management*.

Individual user accounts

AWS provides a centralized web service called AWS IAM for creating and managing individual users within your AWS Account. These users are global entities. They can access their AWS account through the **command line interface (CLI)**, through SDK or API, or through the management console using their credentials. We are going to have a detailed look at IAM in the next chapter.

Secure HTTPS access points

AWS provides API endpoints as a mechanism to securely communicate with their services; for example, `https://dynamodb.us-east-1.amazonaws.com` is an API endpoint for AWS DynamoDB (AWS NoSQL service) for us-east-1 (Northern Virginia) region. These API endpoints are URLs that are entry points for an AWS web service. API endpoints are secure customer access points to employ secure HTTPS communication sessions for enabling better security while communicating with AWS services. HTTPS uses **Secure Socket Layer (SSL) / Transport Layer Security (TLS)** cryptographic protocol that helps prevent forgery, tampering and eavesdropping. The identity of communication parties is authenticated using public key cryptography.

Security logs

Logging is one of the most important security feature of AWS. It helps with auditing, governance and compliance in cloud. AWS provides you with AWS CloudTrail that logs all events within your account, along with the source of that event at 5 minute interval, once it is enabled. It provides you with information such as the source of the request, the AWS service, and all actions performed for a particular event.

AWS CloudTrail logs all API calls such as calls made through AWS CLI, calls made programmatically, or clicks and sign-in events for the AWS Management Console.

AWS CloudTrail will store events information in the form of logs; these logs can be configured to collect data from multiple regions and/or multiple AWS accounts and can be stored securely in one S3 bucket. Moreover, these events can be sent to CloudWatch logs and these logs could be consumed by any log analysis and management tools such as Splunk, ELK, and so on.

Amazon CloudWatch is a monitoring service that has a feature CloudWatch log that can be used to store your server, application and custom log files and monitor them. These log files could be generated from your EC2 instances or other sources such as batch processing applications.

We are going to have a detailed look at the logging feature in AWS along with AWS CloudTrail and Amazon CloudWatch in the subsequent chapters.

AWS Trusted Advisor security checks

The AWS Trusted Advisor customer support service provides best practices or checks across the following four categories:

- Cost optimization
- Fault tolerance
- Security
- Performance

Let us look at alerts provided by the AWS Trusted Advisor for security categories. If there are ports open for your servers in cloud, that opens up possibilities of unauthorized access or hacking; if there are internal users without IAM accounts, or S3 buckets in your account are accessible to the public, or if AWS CloudTrail is not turned on for logging all API requests or if MFA is not enabled on your AWS root account, then AWS Trusted Advisor will raise an alert. AWS Trusted Advisor can also be configured to send you an email every week automatically for all your security alert checks.

The AWS Trusted Advisor service provides checks for four categories; these is, cost optimization, performance, fault tolerance, and security for free of cost to all users, including the following three important security checks:

- Specific ports unrestricted
- IAM use
- MFA on root account

There are many more checks available for each category, and these are available when you sign up for the business or enterprise level AWS support. Some of these checks are as follows:

- Security groups-Unrestricted access
- Amazon S3 bucket permissions
- AWS CloudTrail logging
- Exposed access keys

The following figure depicts the AWS Trusted Advisor checks for an AWS account. We will take a deep dive into the Trusted Advisor security checks later in this book:

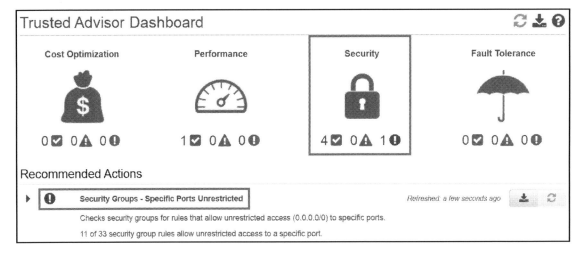

Figure 10 - AWS Trusted Advisor checks

AWS Config security checks

AWS Config is a continuous monitoring and assessment service that records changes in the configuration of your AWS resources. You can view the current and past configurations of a resource and use this information to troubleshoot outages, conduct security attack analysis, and much more. You can view the configuration at time and use that information to reconfigure your resources and bring them into a steady state during an outage situation.

Using Config Rules, you can run continuous assessment checks on your resources to verify that they comply with your own security policies, industry best practices, and compliance regimes such as PCI/HIPAA. For example, AWS Config provides managed Config rules to ensure that encryption is turned on for all EBS volumes in your account. You can also write a custom Config rule to essentially codify your own corporate security policies. AWS Config send you alerts in real time when a resource is wrongly configured, or when a resource violates a particular security policy.

The following figure depicts various rule sets in AWS Config; these could be custom rules or rules provided out of the box by AWS:

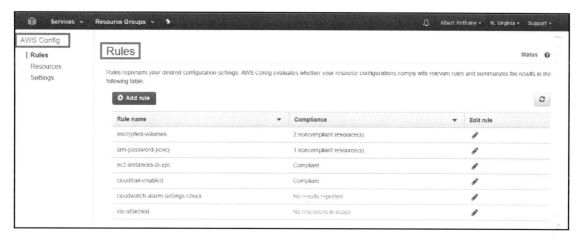

Figure 11 - AWS Config Rules

AWS Security services

Now, let us look at AWS Security services. These are AWS services that primarily provide ways to secure your resources in AWS. We'll briefly go over these services in this section as all of these services are discussed in detail in the subsequent chapters.

AWS Identity and Access Management

AWS IAM enables customers to control access securely for their AWS resources and AWS users. In a nutshell, IAM provides authentication and authorization for accessing AWS resources. It supports accessing AWS resources through a web-based management console, CLI, or programmatically through API and SDK. It has basic features for access control such as users, groups, roles, and permissions as well as advanced features such as Identity Federation for integrating with the customer's existing user database, which could be a Microsoft Active Directory or Facebook, or Google. You can define granular permissions for all your resources as well as use temporary security credentials for providing access to external users outside of your AWS account.

AWS Virtual Private Cloud

AWS VPC is an IaaS that allows you to create your own VPN in the cloud. You can provision your resources in this logically isolated network in AWS. This network can be configured to connect to your on-premise data center securely. You can configure firewalls for all your resources in your VPC at instance level and/or subnet level to control traffic passing in and out of your VPC. VPC has a VPC flow log feature that enables you to collect information regarding IP traffic of your VPC.

AWS Key Management System (KMS)

AWS KMS is a service that helps you manage keys used for encryption. There are multiple options for KMS that include bringing your own keys and having them managed by KMS along with those generated by AWS. This is a fully managed service and integrates with other AWS Services such as AWS CloudTrail to log all activities for your KMS services. This service plays an important role in securing the data stored by your applications by encrypting them.

AWS Shield

AWS shield protects your web applications running on AWS from managed **Distributed Denial of Service (DDoS)** attacks. It is a fully managed service and has two variants, standard and advanced. AWS shield standard is offered to all customers free of charge and provides protection from most common attacks that target your applications or websites on AWS. AWS shield advanced gives you higher levels of protection, integration with other services such as web application firewalls, and access to the AWS DDoS response team.

AWS Web Application Firewall (WAF)

AWS WAF is a configurable firewall for your web applications, allowing you to filter traffic that you want to receive for your web applications. It is a managed service and can be configured either from the management console or through AWS WAF API, so you can have security checkpoints at various levels in your application by multiple actors such as developer, DevOps engineer, security analysts, and so on.

AWS CloudTrail

This is a logging service that logs all API requests in and out of your AWS account. It helps with compliance, auditing, and governance. It delivers a log of API calls to an S3 bucket periodically. This log can be analyzed by using log analysis tools for tracing the history of events. This service plays a very important part in Security Automation and Security Analysis.

AWS CloudWatch

This is a monitoring service that provides metrics, alarms and dashboards for all AWS Services available in your account. It integrates with other AWS services such as AutoScaling, Elastic Load Balancer, AWS SNS, and AWS Lambda for automating response for a metric crossing threshold. It can also collect and monitor logs. AWS CloudWatch can also be used to collect and monitor custom metrics for your AWS resources or applications.

AWS Config

AWS Config is a service that lets you audit and evaluates the configuration of your AWS resources. You can visit the historical configuration of your AWS resources to audit any incident. It helps you with compliance auditing, operational troubleshooting, and so on. You will use this service to make sure your AWS resources stay compliant and configured as per your baseline configuration. This service enables continuous monitoring and continuous assessment of configuration of your AWS resources.

AWS Artifact

This service gives you all compliance related documents at the click of a button. AWS Artificat is a self service, on-demand portal dedicated to compliance and audit related information along with select agreements such as business addendum and non disclosure agreement, and so on.

Penetration testing

AWS allows you to conduct penetration testing for your own EC2 and **Relational Database Service (RDS)** instances; however, you have to first submit a request to AWS. Once AWS approves this request, you can conduct penetration testing and vulnerability scans for EC2 and RDS instances in your AWS account. We'll take a detailed look at penetration testing in subsequent chapters.

AWS Security resources

AWS provides several resources to help you secure your workload on AWS. Let us look at these resources.

AWS documentation

This is one of the best resources available for developers, system administrators, and IT executives alike. It is free, comprehensive, and covers all AWS services including software development kits for various languages and all AWS toolkits. You can find the AWS documentation at `https://aws.amazon.com/documentation`.

AWS whitepapers

These technical white papers are constantly updated with new services, and features added for all services. It is free and covers a wide variety of topics for securing your network, data, security by design, architecture, and so on. These white papers are written by professionals inside and outside of AWS and they are available at `https://aws.amazon.com/whitepapers`.

AWS case studies

AWS has case studies specific to industry, domain, technology, and solutions. They have more than a million active customers across the globe and there are scores of case studies to help you with your use case, irrespective of your industry, or size of your organization. These case studies are available at `https://aws.amazon.com/solutions/case-studies`.

AWS YouTube channel

AWS has numerous events such as AWS Summit, AWS Re:Invent, and so on throughout the year around the globe. There are sessions on security at these events where customer AWS and AWS partners share tips, success stories, ways to secure the network, data, and so on. These videos are uploaded to the AWS channel on YouTube. This is a treasure trove for learning about AWS services from the best in the business. There are multiple channels for various topics and multiple languages. You can subscribe to the AWS YouTube channels at `https://www.youtube.com/channel/UCd6MoB9NC6uYN2grvUNT-Zg`.

AWS blogs

AWS has blogs dedicated to various topics such as AWS Security, AWS big data, AWS DevOps, and so on. There are blogs for countries as well such as, AWS blog (China), AWS blog (Brazil), and so on. There are blogs for technologies such as AWS .NET, AWS PHP, and so on. You can subscribe to these blogs at `https://aws.amazon.com/blogs/aws`.

AWS Partner Network

When you require external help to complete your project on AWS, you can reach out to professionals on the AWS Partner Network. These are organizations authorized by AWS as consulting or technology partners. They can provide professional services to you for your AWS requirements such as security, compliance, and so on. You can find more information about them at `https://aws.amazon.com/partners`.

AWS marketplace

AWS marketplace is an online store where 3500+ products are available that integrate seamlessly with your AWS resources and AWS services. Most of these offer a free trial version of their products and these products are available for security as well as other requirements. We'll have a detailed look at the AWS marketplace in the subsequent chapters. You can visit AWS Marketplace at `https://aws.amazon.com/marketplace`.

Summary

Let us recap what we have learnt in this chapter:

We learnt about the shared security responsibility models of AWS. We found that AWS does the heavy lifting for customers by taking complete ownership of the security of its global infrastructure of regions and availability zones consisting of data centers, and lets customers focus on their business. We got to know that AWS offers multiple services under broad categories and we need to have different security models for various services that AWS offers, such as AWS infrastructure services, AWS container services, and AWS abstract services.

AWS has a different set of security responsibilities for AWS and the customer for the above three categories. We also learnt about physical security of AWS, global infrastructure, network security, platform security, and people and procedures followed at AWS. We looked at ways to protect our AWS account. We went through a couple of AWS services such as AWS Trusted Advisor's and AWS Config and saw how they can help us secure our resources in cloud. We briefly looked at security logs and AWS CloudTrail for finding the root causes for security related incidents. We'll look at logging features in detail in the subsequent chapters later in this book.

In subsequent chapters, we'll go through services that AWS offers to secure your data, applications, network, access, and so on. For all these services, we will provide scenarios and solutions for all the services. As mentioned earlier, the aim of this book is to help you automate security in AWS and help you build security by design for all your AWS resources. We will also look at logging for auditing and identifying security issues within your AWS account. We will go through best practices for each service and we will learn about automating as many solutions as possible.

In the next chapter, *AWS Identity and Access Management*, we will deep dive into AWS IAM that lets you control your AWS resources securely from a centralized location. IAM serves as an entry point to AWS Security where AWS transfers the security baton to customers for allowing tiered access and authenticating that access for all your AWS resources. We are going to see how we can provide access to multiple users for resources in our AWS account. We will take a look at the various credentials available in detail. We will deep dive into AWS identities such as users, groups and roles along with access controls such as permissions and policies.

2
AWS Identity and Access Management

AWS **Identity and Access Management (IAM)** is a web service that helps you securely control access to AWS resources for your users. You use IAM to control who can use your AWS resources (authentication) and what resources they can use and in what ways (authorization).

In other words, or rather a simpler definition of IAM is as follows:

AWS IAM allows you to control who can take what actions on which resources in AWS.

IAM manages users (identities) and permissions (access control) for all AWS resources. It is offered free of charge, so you don't have to pay to use IAM. It provides you greater control, security, and elasticity while working with AWS cloud.

IAM gives you the ability to grant, segregate, monitor, and manage access for multiple users inside your organization or outside of your organization who need to interact with AWS resources such as **Simple Storage Service (S3)** or **Relational Database Service (RDS)** in your AWS account. IAM integrates with AWS CloudTrail, so you can find information in logs about requests made to your resources in your AWS account; this information is based on IAM identities.

IAM is a centralized location for controlling and monitoring access control for all the resources in your AWS account.

Chapter overview

In this chapter, we are going to learn about AWS IAM. We will go through various IAM tools and features and their use cases and look at ways in which we can access IAM. We will deep dive into IAM authentication and authorization. Authentication includes identities such as users, roles, and groups, and authorization talks about access management, permissions, and policies for AWS resources. We'll walk through the benefits of IAM and how it can help us secure our AWS resources. Finally, we'll take a look at IAM best practices.

The following is a snapshot of what we'll cover in this chapter:

- IAM features and tools
- IAM authentication
- IAM authorization
- AWS credentials
- IAM limitations
- IAM best practices

This chapter will help us understand user authentication and access control in detail. Essentially, IAM is our first step towards securing our AWS resources. All of us who have used a laptop or a mobile phone understand that access control plays a vital part in securing our resources. So, if a person gets hold of your credentials, it will be disastrous from the point of view of data security. Ensuring your credentials are secure, having trusted entities interacting with your AWS resources, and having stringent controls as well as greater flexibility allows you to support multiple use cases with a wide variety of AWS resources.

Along with learning about all available IAM features, we will also learn how to create, monitor, and manage various identities, their credentials, and policies. Additionally, we'll look at **Multi-Factor Authentication (MFA)**, **Secure Token Service (STS)**, and tools such as IAM policy simulator.

Following on, we'll deep dive into identities and policies. We'll learn what tools and features are available in AWS IAM to support a myriad of use cases for allowing access and performing actions on AWS resources. We will go through the various credentials that AWS provides and how to manage them.

We'll go through IAM limitations for various entities and objects. Lastly, we'll take a look at IAM best practices that are recommended to ensure that all your resources can be accessed in a secure manner.

IAM features and tools

IAM is free of cost. It is **Payment Card Industry Data Security Standard (PCI-DSS)** compliant, so you can run your credit card application and store credit card information using IAM. It is also eventually consistent, meaning any change you make in IAM would be propagated across multiple AWS data centers: this propagation could take a few milliseconds. So design your application and architecture keeping this feature in mind. IAM integrates with various AWS services so you can define fine grain access control for these services.

Let us look at other features of IAM that make it such a widely used, powerful, and versatile AWS service. As a matter of fact, if you have an AWS account and you want to use resources in your AWS account, you have to pass through IAM in one way or other, there's no two ways about it!

Security

IAM is secure by default. When you create a new user in IAM, by default this user has no permission assigned for any AWS resource. You have to explicitly grant permissions to users for AWS resources and assign them unique credentials. You don't have a need for sharing credentials as you can create separate identities (user accounts) and multiple types of credentials for all use cases.

AWS account shared access

If you are an organization or an enterprise, you would have one or more AWS accounts, and you will have a requirement to allow other people access your AWS account(s). IAM allows you to do that with the help of user accounts without you sharing your credentials with other people. If you are an individual and you want other people to access your AWS account, you can do that as well by creating separate user accounts for them in your AWS account.

Granular permissions

Let's take a common scenario: you want to allow developers in your organization to have complete access to the **Elastic Compute Cloud** (**EC2**) service and the finance or accounting team should have access to billing information and people in the human resources department should have access to a few S3 buckets. You can configure these permissions in IAM, however, let's say you want to have your developers access the EC2 service only from Monday to Friday and between office hours (let's say 8 a.m. to 6 p.m.), you can very well configure that as well.

IAM allows you to have really fine grain permissions for your users and for your resources. You could even allow users to access certain rows and columns in your DynamoDB table!

Identity Federation

At times, you'll have a requirement to allow access to users or resources, such as applications outside of your organization, to interact with your AWS services. To facilitate such requirements, IAM provides a feature called **Identity Federation**. It allows you to provide temporary access to those having their credentials stored outside of your AWS account such as Microsoft Active Directory, Google, and so on. We'll have a detailed look at identity federation later in this chapter.

Temporary credentials

There are scenarios where you would want an entity to access resources in your AWS account temporarily and you do not want to create and manage credentials for them. For such scenarios, IAM offers the roles feature. Roles could be assumed by identities. IAM manages credentials for roles and rotates these credentials several times in a day. We will look at roles in detail in our IAM authentication section in this chapter.

You could access IAM in the following four ways:

- AWS Management Console
- AWS command line tools
- AWS software development kits
- IAM HTTPS API

Let us look at these options in detail:

AWS Management Console

The AWS Management Console is a web based interface for accessing and managing AWS resources and services including IAM. Users are required to sign in using the sign-in link for AWS account along with their username and password. When you create a user, you choose if they can access AWS resources using either the AWS console or by using the AWS command line interface, that is, programmatically or by both methods.

AWS Management Console is available on various devices such as tables and mobile phones. You can also download a mobile app for AWS console from Amazon Apps, iTunes, or Google Play.

As an AWS account owner, you get the URL for the sign-in when you log in to your AWS account. This URL is unique for each account and is used only for web based sign-in. You can customize this URL as well through your AWS account to make it more user friendly.

You can also use your root account credentials for signing-in through the web based interface. Simply navigate to the account sign-in page and click on the **Sign-in using root credentials** link as shown in the following figure. However, as discussed in `Chapter 1`, *Overview of Security in AWS*, AWS does not recommend using your root account for carrying out day to day tasks, instead AWS recommends creating separate user accounts with the required privileges:

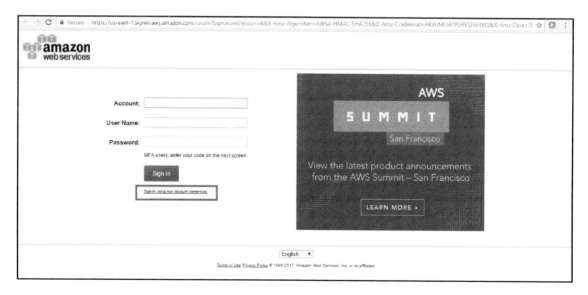

Figure 1 - AWS console login

AWS command line tools

AWS **command line interface (CLI)** and AWS tools for Windows PowerShell are two tools provided by AWS to access AWS services. These tools are specifically useful for automating your tasks through scripts on your system's command line and are often considered more convenient and faster than using AWS Management Console. AWS CLI is available for Windows, Mac, and Linux. You can find more information about AWS CLI including the downloadable version at `https://aws.amazon.com/cli`.

AWS SDKs

AWS **Software Development Kits (SDKs)** are available for popular programming languages such as .NET, JAVA, and so on. AWS SDKs are also available for platforms such as iOS and Android for developing web and mobile applications. These SDKs enables application developers to create applications that can interact with various AWS services by providing libraries, sample code etc. For more information about these SDKs, please visit `https://aws.amazon.com/tools`.

IAM HTTPS API

Another way to programmatically access AWS Services including IAM is to use IAM HTTPS (secure HTTP) **Application Programming Interface (API)**. All the API requests originating from AWS developer tools such as AWS CLI and AWS SDKs are digitally signed by AWS, providing additional layer of security for data in transit.

IAM Authentication

IAM authentication in AWS includes the following identities:

- Users
- Groups
- Roles
- Temporary security credentials
- Account root user

Identities are used to provide authentication for people, applications, resources, services, and processes in your AWS account. Identities represent the user that interacts with the AWS resources based on authentication and authorization to perform various actions and tasks. We will look at each one of the identities in detail.

IAM user

You create an IAM user in AWS as an entity to allow people to sign into the AWS Management Console or to make requests to AWS services from your programs using CLI or API. An IAM user can be a person, an application, or an AWS service that interacts with other AWS services in one way or another. When you create a user in IAM, you provide it with a name and a password that is required to sign into the AWS Management Console. Additionally, you can also provision up to two access keys for an IAM user consisting of the access key ID and a secret access key, that are needed to make requests to AWS from CLI or API.

As we know, by default IAM users have no permissions, so you need to give this brand new user permissions either by assigning them directly or by adding them to a group that has all the necessary permissions, the latter being recommended by AWS and a much preferred way to manage your users and their permissions. Alternatively, you can also clone permissions of an existing IAM user to copy policies and add users to the same groups as the existing IAM users. With every IAM user, there are the following three types of identification options available:

- Every IAM user has a friendly name such as Albert or Jack that's helpful in identifying or associating with people for whom we have created this user account. This name is given when you create an IAM user and it is visible in the AWS Management Console.
- Every IAM user has an **Amazon Resource Name (ARN)** as well; this name is unique for every resource across AWS. An ARN for an IAM user in my AWS account looks like `arn:aws:iam::902891488394:user/Albert`.
- Every IAM user has a unique identifier for the user that's not visible in the AWS Management Console. You can get this ID only when you create a user in the IAM programmatically through API or AWS command line tools such as AWS CLI.

Whenever we create a new IAM user, either through AWS console or programmatically, there aren't any credentials assigned to this user. You have to create credentials for this user based on access requirements. As we have seen earlier, a brand new IAM user does not have any permission to perform any actions in AWS account for any AWS resources. Whenever you create an IAM user, you can assign permissions directly to each individual users. AWS recommends that you follow the least privilege principles while assigning permissions, so if a user named Jack needs to access S3 buckets, that's the only permission that should be assigned to this user.

The following figure shows IAM users for my AWS account:

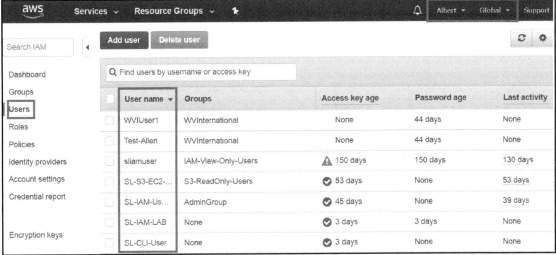

Figure 2 - AWS IAM users

Let us look at the steps to create a new IAM user by using the AWS console. You can also create an IAM user through AWS CLI, IAM HTTP API, or tools for Windows PowerShell:

1. Navigate to the IAM dashboard.
2. Click on the **Users** link. It will show you the existing users (if any) for your AWS account as shown in the preceding figure – AWS IAM users.
3. IAM is a global service so you will see all users in your AWS account.
4. Click on the **Add user** button.
5. Add a friendly name for the user in the username textbox.

6. If this user is going to access AWS through the console then give this user the AWS Management Console Access, if the user will access AWS resources only programmatically then give only programmatic access by selecting the appropriate checkbox. You can select both options as well for a user.

7. Click on the **Permissions** button to navigate to the next page.

8. On the **Permissions** page, you have three options for assigning permissions to this user. You can assign permissions at this stage or you can assign them after you have created this user:

   - You can add this user to a group so the user gets all the permissions attached to a group.
   - You can copy permissions from an existing user so this new user will have the same permissions as an existing use
   - You can attach permissions directly to this user

9. Click on the **Next: Review** button.

10. On this page, review all information for this user that you have entered so far and if all looks good, click on the **Create User** button to create a new IAM user. If you want to edit any information, click on the **Previous** button to go back and edit it.

11. On the next page, you are presented with the success message along with credentials for this user. AWS also provides you with a `.csv` file that contains all credentials for this user. These credentials are available for download only once. If these credentials are lost, they cannot be recovered, however, new credentials can be created anytime.

When you navigate to the **Users** page through the IAM dashboard, on the top right-hand corner, you see **global** written inside a green rectangle. This indicates that users are global entities, that is when you create a user you do not have to specify a region. AWS services in all regions are accessible to an IAM user. Moreover, each IAM user is attached to one AWS account only, it cannot be associated with more than one AWS account. Another thing to note is that you do not need to have separate payment information for your users stored in AWS, all the charges incurred by activities of users in your AWS account is billed to your account.

As noted earlier, an IAM user can be a person, an AWS service, or an application. It is an identity that has permissions to do what it needs to do and credentials to access AWS services as required. You can also create an IAM user to represent an application that needs credentials in order to make requests to AWS. This type of user account is known as a service account. You could have applications with their own service accounts in your AWS account with their own permissions.

IAM groups

A collection of IAM users is known as an IAM group. Groups allow you to manage permissions for more than one users by placing them according to their job functions, departments, or by their access requirements. So, in a typical IT organization, you'll have groups for developers, administrators, and project managers. You will add all users belonging to their job functions in groups and assign permissions directly to the group; all users belonging to that group will get that permission automatically. If a developer moves to another job function within an organization, you'll simply change his/her group to get new permissions and revoke the old ones. Thus making it easier to manage permissions for multiple users in your organization.

Let us look at features of IAM groups:

- A group can have multiple users and a user can be member of more than one group.
- Nesting of group is not allowed, you can't have a group within a group.
- A group can contain many users, and a user can belong to multiple groups.
- Groups can't be nested; they can contain only users, not other groups.
- Groups are not allowed to have security credentials and they can't access AWS services. They simply provide a way to manage IAM users and permissions required for IAM users.
- Groups can be renamed, edited, created, and deleted from AWS console as well as from CLI.

Let us look at the following diagram as an example for IAM groups, there are three groups **Admins**, **Developers**, and **Test**. The Admins group contains two people, Bob and Susan, whereas Developers group contains application such as DevApp1 along with people. Each of these users in these groups have their own security credentials:

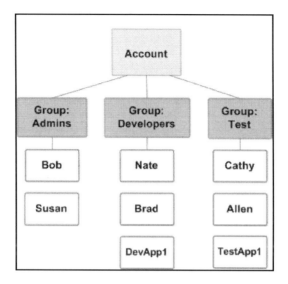

Figure 3 - AWS IAM groups

Normally, the following would be the sequence of events for creating these groups and users:

1. AWS account will be created by the organization.
2. Root user will login and create the Admins group and two users Bob and Susan.
3. Root user will assign administrator permission to Admins group and add Bob and Susan to the Admins group.
4. Users in the Admins group will follow the same process for creating other groups, users, assigning permissions to groups, and adding users to groups.

Note that the root user is used only for creating the admins users and groups. Alternatively, root user can simply create an IAM user Susan with administrator permission and all of the work after that can be done by user Susan. After that, all other groups and users are created by using users who have administrator permissions.

Let us look at the following steps to create groups using AWS console. You can create groups from AWS CLI, AWS API, and tools for Windows PowerShell as well:

1. Navigate to IAM by using the AWS console.
2. Click on **Groups** in the navigation pane.
3. Click on the **Create New Group** button. On this page, you can see all groups present in your AWS account.

4. Give the name for your group and click on the **Next Step** button.

5. On the next page, you can attach a policy to your group or you could do it after you have created a group.

6. Review all the information for this group and click on the **Create Group** button.

7. Once your group is created, you can add/remove users from this group. You can also edit or delete the group from the console.

IAM roles

An IAM role is an AWS identity, recommended by AWS over the IAM user for the many benefits it provides when compared to an IAM user. A role is not necessarily associated with one person, application, or a service, instead, it is assumable by any resource that needs it. Moreover, credentials for roles are managed by AWS; these credentials are created dynamically and rotated multiple times in a day. Roles are a very versatile feature of IAM, it can be used for a variety of use cases such as delegating access to services, applications or users that might not need access to your AWS resources regularly or they are outside of your organization and need to access your AWS resources. You can also provide access to resources whose credentials are stored outside of your AWS account such as your corporate directory. You can have the following scenarios making use of roles:

- An IAM user having different AWS account as the role.
- An IAM user having similar AWS account as IAM role.
- AWS web service provided by AWS such as S3.
- Any user outside of your organization that is authenticated by any external identity provider service compatible with **Security Assertion Markup Language** (**SAML**) 2.0 or OpenID Connect or Compatible with any custom built identity broker.

Let us look at the steps to create a role using the AWS console. You can create roles by using the AWS CLI, AWS API, or tools for Windows PowerShell:

1. Navigate to the IAM dashboard from the AWS console.

2. Click on **Roles** in the navigation pane.

3. Click on the **Create New Role** button. On this screen, you can view, edit, and delete all roles available in your AWS account.

4. Select one of the 4 types of IAM roles available as mentioned in the next section.

5. Attach policies to this role and click on the **Next Step** button.

6. On the next screen, give a user friendly name to this role and optionally add a description.
7. You can also change policies on this screen.
8. Click on the **Create Role** button. It will create this new role.

There are the following four types of IAM roles available in AWS for various use cases:

AWS service role

There are scenarios where an AWS service such as Amazon EC2 needs to perform actions on your behalf, for example, an EC2 instance would need to access S3 buckets for uploading some files, so we'll create an AWS Service Role for EC2 service and assign this role to the EC2 instance. While creating this service role, we'll define all the permissions required by the AWS service to access other AWS resources and perform all actions.

The following figure shows various AWS service roles available in IAM:

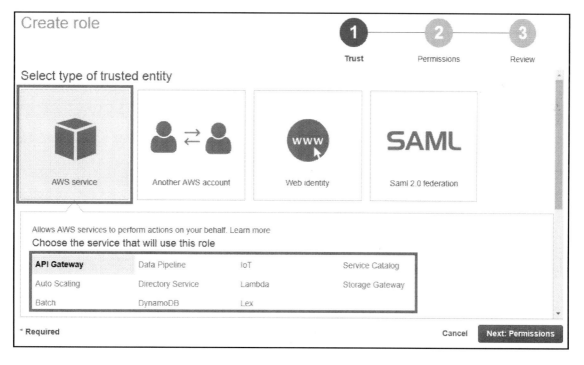

Figure 4 - AWS Service Role types

AWS SAML role

SAML 2.0 (Security Assertion Markup Language 2.0) is an authentication protocol that is most commonly used between an identity provider and service provider. AWS allows you to create roles for SAML 2.0 providers for identity federation. So, if your organization is already using identity provider software that is compatible with SAML 2.0, you can use it to create trust between your organization and AWS as service provider. This will help you create a single sign on solution for all users in your organization.

You can also create your own custom identity provider solution that is compatible with SAML 2.0 and associate it with AWS.

The following figure shows the AWS SAML 2.0 role available in IAM dashboard:

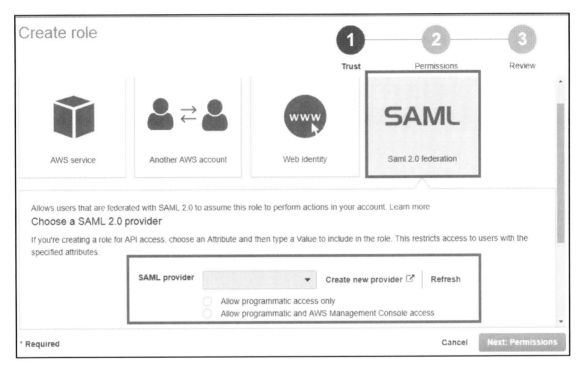

Figure 5 - AWS SAML Role

Role for cross-account access

This role supports two scenarios, the first enabling access between your multiple AWS accounts and the second enabling access to your AWS account by resources in other AWS accounts that are not owned by you. Roles are the primary way to support scenarios for cross-account access and enabling delegation. You can use this role to delegate permissions to another IAM user.

The following figure shows the various options available for cross-account access:

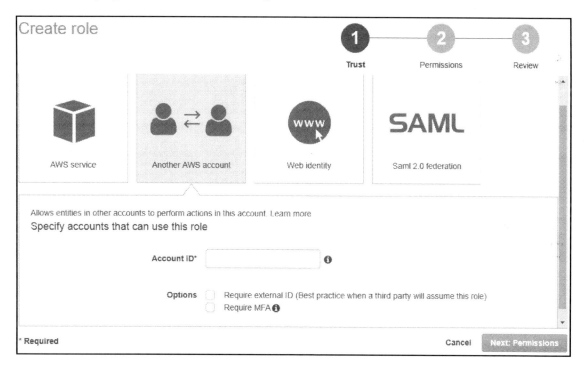

Figure 6 - AWS cross-account access roles

Role for Web Identity Provider

There are times when you will have a requirement to provide access to resources in your AWS account for users who are not authorized to use AWS credentials; instead they use either web identity providers such as Facebook, Amazon, and so on, for sign in or any identity provider compatible with **OpenID Connect (OIDC)**. When users are authenticated by these external web identity providers, they will be assigned an IAM role. These users will receive temporary credentials required to access AWS resources in your AWS account.

The following figure the shows various options available for creating roles for Identity provider access:

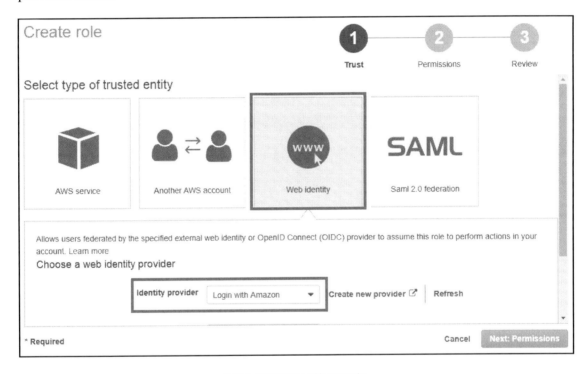

Figure 7 - AWS identity provider access roles

Let us also look at the other terms used with reference to IAM roles.

Identity Provider and Federation

As we have seen earlier, we can manage user identities for our IAM users either in AWS or outside of AWS by using IAM identity providers. You can give access to your AWS resources to the user whose identities are managed by AWS or outside of AWS. This functionality supports scenarios where your users are already managed by your organization's identity management system, such as Microsoft Active Directory. It also supports use cases where an application or a mobile app needs to access your AWS resources.

Identity providers help keep your AWS account secure because your credentials are not embedded in your application. To use an identity provider, you will need to create an IAM identity provider entity to establish a trust relationship between your AWS account and the identity provider. AWS supports two types of identity providers:

- OpenID Connect Compatible
- SAML 2.0 Compatible

You can create an identity provider from the IAM dashboard. This creates trust between your AWS account and identity provider. For more information on how to create identity providers, please visit the following URL:

```
http://docs.aws.amazon.com/IAM/latest/UserGuide/id_roles_providers_create.html
```

Alternatively, if you have users of a mobile application that need access to your AWS resources, you can use the web identity federation. These users can sign in using the already established and popular identity providers such as Facebook, Amazon, Google, and so on and receive an authorization token. This token can be exchanged for temporary security credentials. These credentials will be mapped to an IAM role that will have permissions to access AWS resources.

AWS, however, recommends that for most scenarios, Amazon Cognito should be used instead of web identity federation as it acts as an identity broker and does much of the federation work for you. We will look at Amazon Cognito in the subsequent chapters.

Delegation

Delegation means granting permission to users in another AWS account to allow access to resources that you own in your AWS account. It involves setting up a trust relationship between two AWS accounts. The trusting account owns the resource and the trusted account contains users needing access for resources. The trusted and trusting accounts can be any of the following:

- The same account
- Two accounts that are both under your (organization's) control
- Two accounts owned by separate organizations

For delegation, you start by creating an IAM role with two policies, a permissions policy and a trust policy. The permissions policy takes care of permissions required to perform actions on an AWS resource and the trust policy contains information about trusted accounts that are allowed to grant its users permissions to assume the role.

A trust policy for roles can't have a wildcard (*) as a principal. The trust policy on the role in the trusting account is one-half of the permissions. The other half is a permissions policy attached to the user in the trusted account that allows that user to switch to, or assume the role. A user who assumes a role temporarily gives up his or her own permissions and instead takes on the permissions of the role. The original user permissions are restored when the user stops using the role or exits. An additional parameter external ID helps ensure secure use of roles between accounts that are not controlled by the same organization.

Temporary security credentials

When you have a requirement to create temporary security credentials instead of persistent, long term security credentials, you will use the AWS **Security Token Service (STS)** to create temporary security credentials for users to access your AWS resources. AWS recommends using these credentials over persistent ones as these are more secure and are managed by AWS. Temporary credentials are useful in scenarios that involve identity federation, delegation, cross-account access, and IAM roles. These credentials are almost similar to access key credentials that are created for IAM users except for few a differences as mentioned in the following:

- As the name implies, temporary security credentials are short lived. You can configure them to be valid from a minimum of 15 minutes to a maximum of 36 hour in case of configuring custom identity broker; the default value is 1 hour. Once these credentials expire, AWS no longer recognizes them and all requests for access are declined.
- Unlike access keys that are stored locally with the user, temporary security credentials are not stored with the user. Since they are managed by AWS, they are generated dynamically and provided to the user when requested, following the principle of last minute credential. The user can request these credentials when they expire or before they expire as long as this user has permissions to request them.

These differences give the following advantages for using temporary credentials:

- You do not have to distribute or embed long-term AWS Security credentials with an application. So, you do not risk losing security credentials if your application is compromised.
- You can provide access to your AWS resources to users without creating an AWS identity for them. It helps keep your user management lean. Temporary credentials are the basis for roles and identity federation.
- The temporary security credentials have a limited lifetime and they are not reusable once they expire. You don't have to worry about defining a credentials policy or ensure if they are rotated periodically, as these tasks are taken care of by AWS internally. You also don't have to plan on revoking them as they are short lived.

AWS Security Token Service

The AWS STS is a web service that enables you to request temporary, limited privilege credentials for IAM users or for users that you authenticate (federated users) to use. Essentially, temporary security credentials are generated by AWS STS.

By default, AWS STS is a global service with a single endpoint at `https://sts.amazonaws.com`, this endpoint points to the US-East-1 (Northern Virginia) region. You can use STS in other regions as well that support this service. This will help you to reduce latency by sending requests to regions closer to you/your customers. Credentials generated by any region are valid globally. If you don't want any region to generate credentials, you can disable it.

AWS STS supports AWS CloudTrail, so you can record and analyze information about all calls made to AWS STS, including who made requests, how many were successful, and so on.

When you activate a region for an account, you enable the STS endpoints in that region to issue temporary credentials for users and roles in that account when a request is made to an endpoint in the region. The credentials are still recognized and are usable globally. It is not the account of the caller, but the account from which the temporary credentials are requested that must activate the region.

AWS STS is offered to all AWS users at no additional charge. You are charged only for services accessed by users having temporary security credentials that are obtained through AWS STS.

The account root user

The account root user is a user that is created when you first create an AWS account using an email id and password. This user has complete access to all AWS services and all resources for this AWS account. This single sign-in identity is known as the root user.

AWS strongly recommends that you do not use the root user for your everyday tasks, even the administrative ones. Instead, use the root account to create your first IAM user and use this first IAM user for all the tasks such as creating additional users or accessing AWS services and resources. AWS recommends that you should delete your root access keys and activate MFA for root user. Root user should be used for performing handful of tasks that specifically require you to use root user. Following are some of such tasks:

- Changing your root account information, such as changing the root user password
- Updating your payment information
- Updating your support plan
- Closing your AWS account

You can find detailed lists of all tasks at http://docs.aws.amazon.com/general/latest/gr/aws_tasks-that-require-root.html.

The following figure shows the IAM dashboard along with recommendations for the account root user:

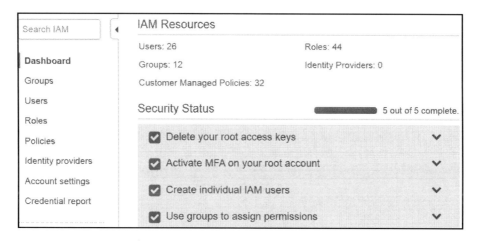

Figure 8 - AWS account root user recommendations

IAM Authorization

When you create an AWS account, it has a user known as root user. This user has, by default, access to all AWS service and resources. No other user (or any IAM entity) has any access by default and we have to explicitly grant access for all users. In this section, we'll talk about authorization in IAM or access management, it is made up of the following two components:

- Permissions
- Policy

Permissions

Permissions let you take actions on AWS resources. It allows your users (AWS identities) to perform tasks in AWS. When you create a new user (except for the root user), it has no permission to take any action in AWS. You grant permissions to the user by attaching a policy to that user. So, for example, you can give permission to a user to access certain S3 buckets or to launch an EC2 instance.

Permissions can be assigned to all AWS identities such as users, groups, and roles. When you give permission to a group, all members of that group get that permission and if you remove a permission from a group, it is revoked from all members of that group.

You can assign permissions in couple of ways:

- **Identity-based**: These permissions are assigned to AWS identities such as users, groups, and roles. They can either be managed or inline (we'll talk about managed and inline in our *Policies* section).
- **Resource-based**: These permissions are assigned to AWS resources such as Amazon S3, Amazon EC2. Resource-based permissions are used to define who has access to an AWS resource and what actions they can perform on it. Resource-based policies are inline only, not managed.

Let us look at examples for each of them:

- **Identity-based**: These permissions are given to identities such as IAM users or groups. For example, there are two IAM users, Albert and Mary. Both have permissions to read S3 buckets and provision EC2 instances.
- **Resource-based**: These permissions are given to AWS resources, such as S3 buckets or EC2 instances. For example, an S3 buckets has allowed access for Albert and Mary; an EC2 service is allowing access for Albert and Mary to provision EC2 instances.

Note that resource-based and resource level permissions are different. Resource-based permissions can be attached directly to a resource whereas resource level goes a level deeper by giving you the ability to manage what actions can be performed by users as well as which resources those actions can be performed upon.

Some AWS services lets you specify permissions for actions such as list, read, write and so on, but they don't let you specify the individual resources such as EC2, S3, RDS and so on. There are a handful of AWS services that support resource-based permissions such as EC2, **Virtual Private Cloud** (**VPC**) and so on.

The following are six IAM permission types that are evaluated for integration with each AWS service:

- **Action-level permissions**: The service supports specifying individual actions in a policy's action element. If the service does not support action-level permissions, policies for the service use wildcard (*) in the Action element.

- **Resource-level permissions**: The service has one or more APIs that support specifying individual resources (using ARNs) in the policy's resource element. If an API does not support resource-level permissions, then that statement in the policy must use * in the `Resource` element.

- **Resource-based permissions**: The service enables you to attach policies to the service's resources in addition to IAM users, groups, and roles. The policies specify who can access that resource by including a `Principal` element.

- **Tag-based permissions**: The service supports testing resource tags in a condition element.

- **Temporary security credentials**: The service lets users make requests using temporary security credentials that are obtained by calling AWS STS APIs like `AssumeRole` or `GetFederationToken`.

- **Service linked roles**: The service requires that you use a unique type of service role that is linked directly to the service. This role is pre-configured and has all the permissions required by the service to carry out the task.

A detailed list of all services that IAM integrates with is available at the following URL:

```
http://docs.aws.amazon.com/IAM/latest/UserGuide/reference_aws-services-that-
work-with-iam.html
```

Many AWS services need to access other AWS services, for example, EC2 might need to access a bucket on S3 or EC2 might need to access an instance on RDS. They need to configure permissions to perform such access, this configuration is provided in detail in the documentation of AWS services.

Policy

A policy is a document listing permissions in the form of statements. It is a document in **JavaScript Object Notation (JSON)** format. It is written according to the rules of the IAM policy language which is covered in the next section. A policy can have one or more statements, with each statement describing one set of permissions. These policies can be attached to any IAM identities such as users, roles, or groups. You can attach more than one policy to an entity. Each policy has its own **Amazon Resource Name (ARN)** that includes the policy name and is an entity in IAM.

Fundamentally, a policy contains information about the following three components:

- **Actions**: You can define what actions you will allow for an AWS service. Each AWS service has its own set of actions. So, for example, you allow the describe-instances action for your EC2 instances, that describes one or more instances based on the instance-id passed as a parameter. If you do not explicitly define an action it is denied by default.
- **Resources**: You need to define what resources actions can be performed on. For example, do you want to allow the describe-instances action on one specific instance or range of instances or all instances. You need to explicitly mention resources in a policy, by default, no resources are defined in a policy.
- **Effect**: You define what the effect will be when a user is going to request access, and there are two values that you can define: allow or deny. By default, access to resources are denied for users, so you would normally specify allow for this component.

The following is a sample policy used to allow all describe actions for all EC2 instances:

```
{
  "Version": "2012-10-17",
  "Statement": [
  {
  "Effect": "Allow",
  "Action": "ec2:Describe*",
  "Resource": "*"
  }
  ]
  }
```

Let us look at the following important elements of a policy.

Statement

The Statement element is the most important and required element for a policy. It can include multiple elements and it can also have nesting of elements. The Statement element contains an array of individual statements. Each individual statement is a JSON block enclosed in braces { }.

Effect

This element is required as well. It specifies if an action is allowed or denied; it has only two valid values, allow, and deny. As mentioned earlier, by default, the value is deny, you have to explicitly allow it.

Principal

A `Principal` element is used to define the user. A user can be an IAM user, federated user, role using user, any AWS account, any AWS service, or any other AWS entity that is allowed or denied access to a resource and that can perform actions in your AWS account. You use the `Principal` element in the trust policies for IAM roles and in resource-based policies.

A `Principal` element should not be used while creating policies that are attached to IAM users or groups and when you are creating an access policy for an IAM role. This is because in these policies a principal is a user or role that is going to use the policy. Similarly, for a group, a principal is an IAM user making the request from that group. A group cannot be identified as a principal because a group is not truly an identity in IAM. It provides a way to attach policies to multiple users at one time.

A principal is specified by using the ARN of the user (IAM user, AWS account, and so on). You can specify more than one user as the `Principal` as shown in the following code:

```
"Principal": {
 "AWS": [
"arn:aws:iam::AWS-account-ID:user/user-name-1",
 "arn:aws:iam::AWS-account-ID:user/UserName2"
 ]
}
```

Action

The `Action` element defines an action or multiple actions that will either be allowed or denied. The statements must include either an `Action` or `NotAction` element. This should be one of the actions each AWS service has; these actions describe tasks that can be performed with that service. For example: `Action": "ec2:Describe*`, is an action.

You can find a list of actions for all AWS services in the API reference documentation available at the following URL:

```
https://aws.amazon.com/documentation/
```

Resource

The `Resource` element describes an AWS resource that the statement cover. All statements must include either a `Resource` or `NotResoruce` element. Every AWS service comes with its own set of resources and you define this element using ARN.

Condition

The `Condition` element also known as condition block lets you provide conditions for a policy. You can create expressions with Boolean condition operators (equal, not equal, and so on.) to match the condition in the policy against values in the request. These condition values can include the date, time, the IP address of the requester, the ARN of the request source, the user name, user ID, and the user agent of the requester. A value from the request is represented by a key.

Whenever a request is made, the policy is evaluated and AWS replaces key with a similar value from the request. The condition returns a boolean value, either true or false, that decides if the policy should either allow or deny that request.

Policies can be categorized into 2 broad categories as follows:

1. **Managed policies**: These are standalone policies that can be attached to IAM identities in your AWS account such as users, groups, and roles. These policies cannot be applied to AWS resources such as EC2 or S3. When you browse through policies on IAM dashboard, you can identify AWS managed policies by the yellow AWS symbol before them. AWS recommends that you use managed policies over inline policies. There are two types of managed policies available:
   - **AWS managed policies**: As the name suggests, these policies are created as well as managed by AWS. To begin with, it is recommended you use AWS managed policies as it will cover almost all of your use cases. You can use these policies to assign permissions to AWS identities for common job functions such as `Administrators`, `SecurityAudit`, `Billing`, `SupportUser`, and so on, as shown in the following figure. AWS managed policies cannot be changed.

- **customer managed policies**: These are the policies created and managed by you in your AWS account. You would normally create a policy when you have a use case that's not supported by an AWS managed policy. You can copy an existing policy, either an AWS managed policy or a customer managed policy and edit it, or you can start from scratch as well to create a policy:

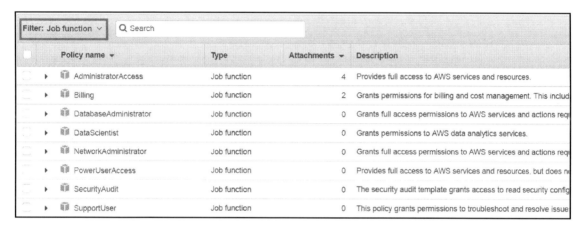

	Policy name ▼	Type	Attachments ▼	Description
▶	AdministratorAccess	Job function	4	Provides full access to AWS services and resources.
▶	Billing	Job function	2	Grants permissions for billing and cost management. This includ
▶	DatabaseAdministrator	Job function	0	Grants full access permissions to AWS services and actions requ
▶	DataScientist	Job function	0	Grants permissions to AWS data analytics services.
▶	NetworkAdministrator	Job function	0	Grants full access permissions to AWS services and actions requ
▶	PowerUserAccess	Job function	0	Provides full access to AWS services and resources, but does no
▶	SecurityAudit	Job function	0	The security audit template grants access to read security config
▶	SupportUser	Job function	0	This policy grants permissions to troubleshoot and resolve issue

Figure 9 - AWS job functions policies

2. **Inline policies**: These are policies created and managed by you, and these policies are embedded directly into a principal entity such as a single user, group, or role. The policy is part of that entity either when you create an entity or you can embed the policy later as well. These policies are not reusable. Moreover, if you delete the principal entity, the inline policy gets deleted as well. You would normally create inline policies when you need to maintain a one to one relationship between a policy and a principal entity, that is, you want to make sure your principal entity is used for a specific purpose only.

Creating a new policy

AWS gives you multiple options to create a new policy in IAM. You can copy an existing AWS managed policy and customize it according to your requirements. You can use the policy generator or you can write JSON code to create a policy from scratch or use the policy editor to create a new policy.

Here are the following common steps to be followed before we choose one of the options for creating a policy:

1. Sign in to the AWS Management Console using your sign in URL.
2. Navigate to the IAM dashboard.
3. Click on **Policies** on the left navigation bar.
4. Click on the **Create Policy** button.
5. Click on any of the three options to create a new policy as shown in the following figure:
   - **Copy an AWS Managed Policy**
   - **Policy Generator**
   - **Create Your Own Policy**

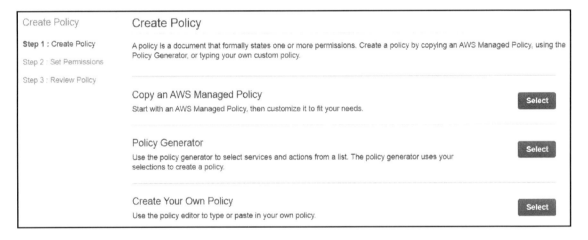

Figure 10 - AWS Create Policy options

IAM Policy Simulator

AWS provides you with a Policy Simulator tool that is accessible at `https://policysim.aws.amazon.com`. IAM Policy Simulator helps you to test as well as troubleshoot policies, both identity and resource based. This tool is quite helpful in testing the scope of existing policies and the scope of newly created policies. You can find out if a policy is allowing or denying the requested actions for a particular service for a selected IAM identity (user, group, or role). Since it is a simulator, it does not make an actual AWS request. This tool is accessible to all users who can access the AWS Management Console.

You can also simulate IAM policies using the AWS CLI, API requests or through tools for Windows PowerShell. You can find more information on testing policies by using the policy simulator at `http://docs.aws.amazon.com/IAM/latest/UserGuide/access_policies_testing-policies.html`. As shown in the following figure, the IAM policy simulator shows for an IAM administrator group how many permissions are allowed or denied for Amazon SQS and AWS IAM services:

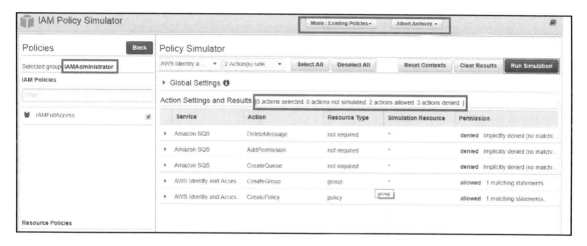

Figure 11 - AWS IAM Policy Simulator

IAM Policy Validator

This is another tool available to fix your non compliant policies in IAM. You will know that you have a non-compliant policy if you see a yellow banner titled Fix policy syntax at the top of the console screen. You can use IAM policy validator only if your policy is not complying with the IAM policy grammar. For example, the size of policy can range between 2048 characters and 10,240 characters excluding the white space characters, or individual elements such as `Statement` cannot have multiple instances of the same key such as `Effect` element. Note that a policy cannot be saved if it fails validation. Policy Validator only checks the JSON syntax and policy grammar, it does not check variables such as ARN or condition keys. You can access policy validator in three ways: while creating policies, while editing policies, and while viewing policies.

Access Advisor

IAM console gives you information on policies that were accessed by a user. This information is very useful to implement the least privilege principle for assigning permissions to your resources. Through access advisor, you can find out what permissions are used infrequently or permissions that are never used, you can then revoke these permissions to improve the security of your AWS account. The following figure shows a few policies in the access advisor that were last accessed 144 days back; there is no reason these policies should be attached to this user:

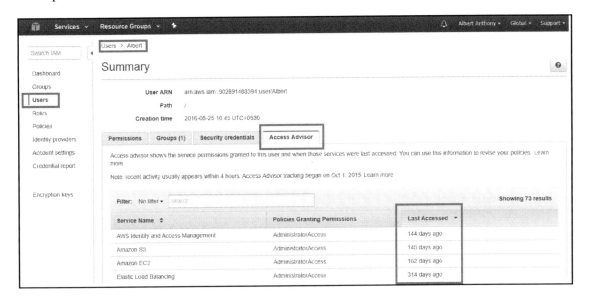

Figure 12 - AWS IAM Access Advisor

Passwords Policy

You can set up the password policy for your AWS account from IAM. Navigate to the IAM dashboard from the AWS console. Click on **Account settings**. As shown in the following figure, on the **Password Policy** page, you can setup requirements such as minimum password length, rotation period, and so on. Most of these changes in your password policy are effective when your users log in the next time, however, for changes such as change in the password expiration period, they are applied immediately:

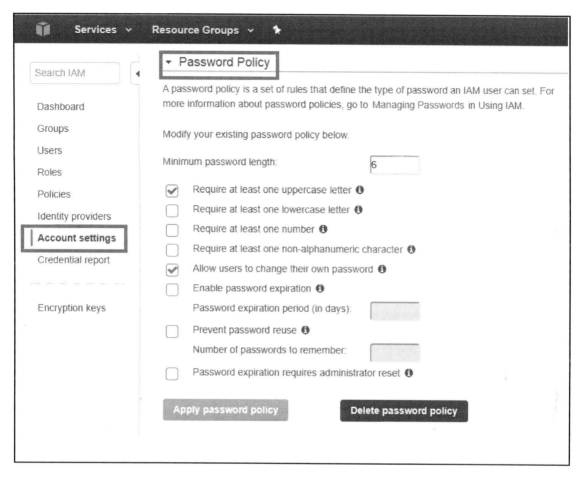

Figure 13 - AWS IAM Password Policy

AWS credentials

As we have seen in the previous chapter, AWS provides you with various credentials to authorize and authenticate your requests. Let us look at these AWS credentials in detail:

- **Email and password**: These credentials are used by your account root user. As discussed earlier, by default, the account root user has access to all services and resources. AWS recommends that root user credentials should be used to create another user and all the work should be carried out by the other user.

- **IAM username and password**: When you create one or more users in your AWS account through IAM. They can login to the AWS console by using the username and password. This username is given by you when you create a user in IAM. Passwords for these users are created by you as well, you can give permissions to users to change their passwords.
- **Multi-factor Authentication (MFA)**: MFA adds an additional layer of security for your AWS account. When you login to the AWS console by using your username and password or by using your email address and password for your root user, you can opt for MFA as an additional level of authentication. You can setup MFA on the hardware device or you can have a virtual token as well. AWS recommends to setup MFA for your account root user and IAM users with higher permissions, to secure your account and resources. You can configure MFA from the IAM console.
- **Access keys (access key ID and secret access key)**: Access keys are used to sign requests sent to AWS programmatically through AWS SDKs or API. AWS SDKs use these access keys to sign requests on your behalf so you don't have to do it yourself. Alternatively, you can sign these requests manually. These keys are used through CLIs. You can either issue commands signed using your access keys or you can store these keys as a configuration setting on your resource sending requests to AWS. You can opt for access keys for users when you are creating them or later through the IAM console.
- **Key pairs**: Key pairs constitutes a public key and a private key. The private key is used to create a digital signature and AWS uses the corresponding public key to validate this digital signature. These key pairs are used only for Amazon EC2 and Amazon CloudFront. They are used to access Amazon EC2 instances, for example, to remotely logging into a Linux instance. For CloudFront, you will use key pairs to create signed URLs for private content, that is when you want to distribute content that can be viewed only by selected people and not by everybody. For EC2, you can create key pairs using the AWS console, CLI, or API. For CloudFront, key pairs can be created only by using the account root user and through the **Security Credentials Page** accessible through the AWS console.
- **AWS account identifiers**: AWS provides two unique IDs for each account that serves as an account identifier: AWS account ID and a canonical user ID. AWS account ID is a 12 digit number, such as `9028-1054-8394` that is used for building ARN. So when you refer to AWS resources in your account such as the S3 bucket, this account ID helps to distinguish your AWS resources from the AWS resources of other accounts. The canonical user ID is a long string such as `28783b48a1be76c5f653317e158f0daac1e92667f0e47e8b8a904e03225b81b5`. You would normally use the canonical user ID if you want to access AWS resources in AWS accounts other than your AWS account.

- **X.509 Certificates**: A X.509 certificate is a security device designed to carry a public key and bind that key to an identity. X.509 certificates are used in public key cryptography. You can either use the certificate generated by AWS or upload your own certificate to associate it with your AWS account.

You can view all these security credentials except for EC2 key pairs in the AWS console as shown in the following figure. The EC2 key pairs can be found on the EC2 dashboard:

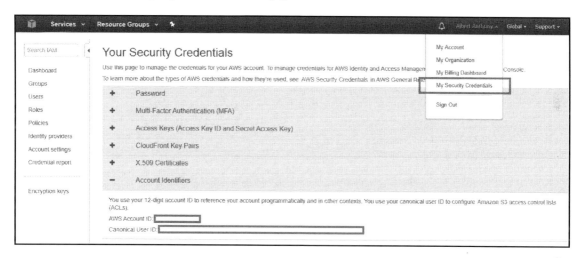

Figure 14 - AWS Security Credentials

IAM limitations

IAM has certain limitations for entities and objects. Let us look at the most important limitations across the most common entities and objects:

- Names of all IAM identities and IAM resources can be alphanumeric. They can include common characters such as plus (+), equal (=), comma (,), period (.), at (@), underscore (_), and hyphen (-).
- Names of IAM identities (users, roles, and groups) must be unique within the AWS account. So you can't have two groups named DEVELOPERS and developers in your AWS account.
- AWS account ID aliases must be unique across AWS products in your account. It cannot be a 12 digit number.

- You can create 100 groups in an AWS account.
- You can create 5000 users in an AWS account. AWS recommends the use of temporary security credentials for adding a large number of users in an AWS account.
- You can create 500 roles in an AWS account.
- An IAM user can be a member of up to 10 groups.
- An IAM user can be assigned a maximum of 2 access keys.
- An AWS account can have a maximum of 1000 customer managed policies.
- You can attach a maximum of 10 managed policies to each IAM entity (user, groups, or roles).
- You can store a maximum of 20 server certificates in an AWS account.
- You can have up to 100 SAML providers in an AWS account.
- A policy name should not exceed 128 characters.
- An alias for an AWS account ID should be between 3 and 63 characters.
- A username and role name should not exceed 64 characters.
- A group name should not exceed 128 characters.

For more information on AWS IAM limitations, please visit http://docs.aws.amazon.com/ IAM/latest/UserGuide/reference_iam-limits.html.

To increase limits for some of these resources, you can contact AWS support through the AWS console.

IAM best practices

Lock root account keys: As we know the root account user has access to all resources for all AWS services by default, so if you have access keys (access key ID and secret access key) for a root account user, lock them in a secure place and rotate them periodically.

Do not share credentials: AWS gives you multiple ways for your users to interact with resources in your AWS account, so you would never have a requirement to share credentials. Create individual users for all access requirements with necessary credentials and never share credentials with other users.

Use managed policies: AWS provides comprehensive sets of policies that cover access requirements for the most common scenarios. AWS also provides you policies aligned with job functions. These policies are managed by AWS and they are updated as and when required so you don't have to worry about your policies getting outdated when new services or functionalities are introduced.

Use groups to manage users: Groups are an excellent way to manage permissions for your users and individual IAM users as well. Always add users to groups and assign policies directly to groups instead of assigning permissions to individual IAM users. Whenever there is a movement required for an individual user, you can simply move them to the appropriate group.

Follow the least privilege principle: Whenever you grant permissions, follow the standard security advice of Least Privilege, that is, if a user does not need to interact with a resource, do not grant access to that resource. Another example of least privilege is that if a user needs read-only access for one S3 bucket, access should be given only for that one S3 bucket and that access should be read-only. Use the IAM Access Advisor feature periodically to verify if all permissions assigned to a user are used frequently. If you find that a permission is used rarely or not used at all, revoke it after confirming it is not required to carry on regular tasks by your IAM user.

Review IAM permissions: Use the IAM summary feature in IAM console to review permissions assigned for each IAM user. Check their access levels for all resources they are allowed to interact with. Access level for a policy is categorized as list, read, write, and permissions management. Review these periodically for all policies. The following image shows how policies are summarized in three categories:

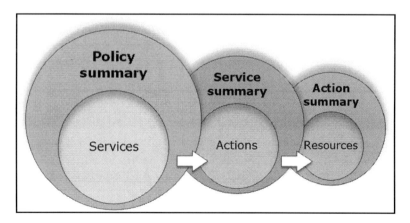

Figure 15 - AWS IAM policy summaries

Enforce strong passwords: Configure your account password policy from **Account settings** in your IAM console to enforce strong passwords for all your users, including periodic password rotation, avoiding reuse of old passwords, minimum length, using alphanumeric characters, and so on.

Enable MFA: Enable MFA for all IAM users who access AWS resources through the AWS Management Console. This will provide an additional layer of security for your AWS resources.

Use roles for applications: For all the applications that run on Amazon EC2 instances, use roles for providing access to other AWS services. Roles are managed by AWS and they do not need to store security credentials on EC2 instances. So, even if your EC2 instance is compromised, your credentials are secure. You can either assign roles to an EC2 instance when you are launching it or you can also assign roles on the fly, that is, when you need to access a resource you can assign it.

Use roles for delegation: Whenever you have a requirement for delegation, that is, you need to allow cross account access, use roles instead of sharing credentials. In general, AWS recommends using roles instead of using individual IAM users as roles are managed by AWS and credentials are rotated several times in a day.

Rotate credentials: Ensure that all credentials in your AWS account are rotated periodically. These credentials include passwords, access keys, key pairs, and so on. This will ensure that you will limit the abuse of your compromised credentials. If you find that credentials are not required for a user, remove them. You can find if credentials are used or not by downloading the credentials report from the AWS console for your AWS account.

Use policy condition: For all policies that allow access, use policy condition element as much as possible. For example: if you know all the IP addresses that should be accessing your AWS resource, add them to the policy condition. Similarly, if you know that you want to allow access only for a limited duration, like for four hours, add that duration to the policy condition. For high privilege actions, such as deleting an S3 bucket or provisioning an EC2 or and RDS instance, enforce **Multi-Factor Authentication (MFA)** by adding it to the policy condition.

Monitor account activity: IAM integrated with AWS CloudTrail that records all API activity for your AWS account. Use AWS CloudTrail to monitor all activities in your account. How many requests where made, how many were allowed and how many were denied. Monitor what actions were performed on your AWS resources and by whom. You can identify suspicious activity from CloudTrail logs and take the necessary actions based on your analysis.

Summary

This concludes Chapter 2, *AWS Identity and Access Management*. IAM is one of the most important AWS service as it controls access to your AWS resources. We had a detailed view of Identities including users, groups, and roles. We learnt how to create each of these identities and what features each of these identities offer to support multiple use cases.

We looked at identity federation to allow access for identities that are managed out of our AWS account. We learnt about delegation, temporary security credentials, AWS Security token service and account root user.

We also learnt about policies and permissions. We went through various elements of a policy. We got to know that AWS managed policies are preferred over inline policies for most use cases. There are multiple tools and features available to help us write, validate, and manage our own policies such as IAM policy validator, access advisor, credentials report, and so on.

Apart from these, we looked at various AWS credentials to support numerous scenarios. We ran through IAM limitations for various entities and objects. Lastly, we went through IAM best practices to secure our AWS resources.

In the next chapter, *AWS Virtual Private Cloud*, we are going to learn how we can secure our network in AWS. VPC, as it is popularly called, closely, resembles your on-premises network and has all the components similar to your on-premises network. So, you will find route tables, subnets, gateways, virtual private connections, and so on available at your fingertips in AWS as well to design your own virtual private network in AWS. We will learn how to create a VPC including various components of a VPC, how to configure it to secure our resources in our VPC, how to connect our network in cloud to our data center securely, and what security features are available for our VPC.

3

AWS Virtual Private Cloud

Amazon Virtual Private Cloud or VPC, as it is popularly known, is a logically separated, isolated, and secure virtual network on the cloud, where you provision your infrastructure, such as Amazon RDS instances and Amazon EC2 instances. It is a core component of networking services on AWS cloud.

A VPC is dedicated to your AWS account. You can have one or more VPCs in your AWS account to logically isolate your resources from each other. By default, any resource provisioned in a VPC is not accessible by the internet unless you allow it through AWS-provided firewalls. A VPC spans an AWS region.

VPC is essentially your secure private cloud within AWS public cloud. It is specifically designed for users who require an extra layer of security to protect their resources on the cloud. It segregates your resources with other resources within your AWS account. You can define your network topology as per your requirements, such as if you want some of your resources hidden from public or if you want resources to be accessible from the internet.

Getting the design of your VPC right is absolutely critical for having a secure, fault-tolerant, and scalable architecture.

It resembles a traditional network in a physical data center in many ways, for example, having similar components such as subnets, routes, and firewalls; however, it is a software-defined network that performs the job of data centers, switches, and routers. It is primarily used to transport huge volume of packets into, out of, and across AWS regions in an optimized and secured way along with segregating your resources as per their access and connectivity requirements. And because of these features, VPC does not need most of the traditional networking and data center gear.

VPC gives you granular control to define what traffic flows in or out of your VPC.

Chapter overview

In this chapter, we will deep dive into the security of AWS VPC. VPC is the most important component of networking services in AWS. Networking services are one of the foundation services on the AWS cloud. A secure network is imperative to ensure security in AWS for your resources.

We will look at components that make up VPC, such as subnets, security groups, various gateways, and so on. We will take a deep dive into the AWS VPC features and benefits such as simplicity, security, multiple connectivity options, and so on.

We will look at the following most popular use cases of VPC that use various security and connectivity features of VPC:

- Hosting a public-facing website
- Hosting multi-tier web applications
- Creating branch office and business unit networks
- Hosting web applications in AWS cloud that are connected with your data center
- Extending corporate network on the cloud
- Disaster recovery

AWS provides multiple measures to secure resources in VPC and monitor activities in VPC, such as security groups, network **access control list** (**ACL**), and VPC flow logs. We will dive deep into each of these measures.

Next, we'll walk through the process of creating a VPC. You can either choose to create a VPC through the wizard, through the console, or through the CLI.

Furthermore, we'll go through the following VPC connectivity options along with VPC limits in detail:

- Network to AWS VPC
- AWS VPC to AWS VPC
- Internal user to AWS VPC

We'll wrap up this chapter with VPC best practices.

Throughout this chapter, we'll take a look at AWS architecture diagrams for various use cases, connectivity options, and features. The objective of this chapter is to familiarize you with AWS VPC and let you know about ways to secure your VPC.

VPC components

AWS VPC is a logically separated network isolated from other networks. It lets you set your own IP address range and configure security settings and routing for all your traffic. AWS VPC is made up of several networking components, as shown in the following figure; some of them are as follows:

- Subnets
- Elastic network interfaces
- Route tables
- Internet gateways
- Elastic IP addresses
- VPC endpoints
- NAT
- VPC peering

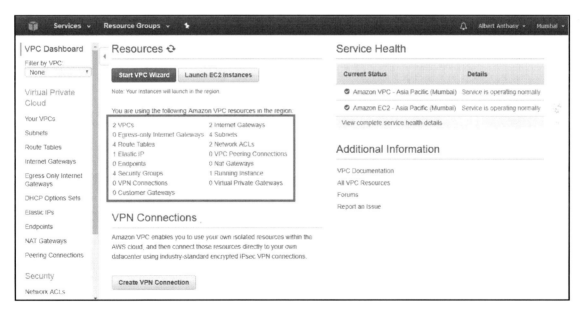

Figure 1 - AWS VPC components

Let's take a closer look at these components:

Subnets

A VPC spans an AWS region. A region contains two or more availability zones. A VPC contains subnets that are used to logically separate resources inside a region. A subnet cannot span across multiple availability zones. A subnet can either be a private subnet or a public subnet based on its accessibility from outside of VPC and if it can access resources outside of VPC.

Subnets are used for separating resources, such as web servers and database servers. They are also used for making your application highly available and fault-tolerant. By default, all resources in all subnets of a VPC can route (communicate) to each other using private IP addresses.

Elastic Network Interfaces (ENI)

The ENI are available for EC2 instances running inside a VPC. An ENI can have many attributes, such as a primary private IPv4 address, a MAC address, one or more security groups, one or more IPv6 addresses, and so on. These attributes will move with ENI when an ENI is attached to an instance; when this ENI is detached from an instance, these attributes will be removed.

By default, every VPC has a network interface attached to every instance. This ENI is known as a primary network interface (eth0). This default ENI cannot be detached from an instance. You can, however, create and attach many additional ENIs to your instances inside a VPC.

One of the popular use cases of ENI is having secondary ENI attached to instances running network and security appliances, such as network address translation servers or load balancers. These ENIs can be configured with their own attributes, such as public and private IP address, security groups, and so on.

Route tables

As you've learned about VPC, it essentially facilitates traffic in and out of a software-defined network. This traffic needs to know where to go, and this is achieved via route tables. A route table in VPC has rules or routes defined for the flow of traffic. Every VPC has a default route table that is known as the main route table. You can modify this main route table and you can create additional route tables.

Each subnet in VPC is associated with only one route table, however, one route table can be attached to multiple subnets. You use route tables to decide what data stays inside of VPC and what data should go outside of VPC, and that is where it plays a very important part in deciding data flow for a VPC.

In the following figure, you can see four route tables for two VPCs in my AWS account. You can see rules in the route table, and you see tabs for subnet associations as well:

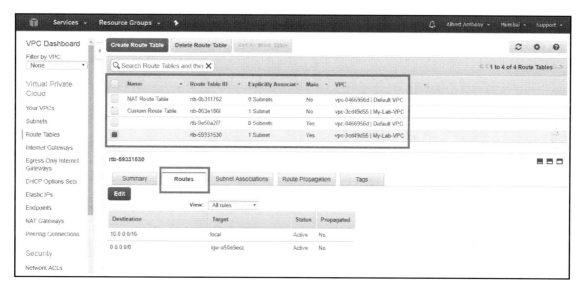

Figure 2 - AWS VPC route tables

Internet Gateway

An internet gateway allows communication between resources such as EC2 and RDS instances in your VPC and the Internet. It is highly available, redundant, and horizontally scalable; that is, you do not need to attach more than one internet gateway to your VPC in order to support an increase in traffic.

An internet gateway serves as a target for route table in VPC for all the traffic that is supposed to go out of VPC to the internet. Along with that, it also performs network address translation for all instances with public IPv4 addresses.

Elastic IP addresses

An Elastic IP Address is a public IPv4, static address that can be associated with any one instance or one network interface at a time within any VPC in your AWS account. When your application is dependent on an IP address, you would use an Elastic IP address instead of a regular public IP address because public IP addresses would be lost if the underlying instance shuts down for some reason. You can simply move your Elastic IP address to another instance that is up and running from a failed instance.

You first allocate an Elastic IP address and then associate it with your instance or network interface. Once you do not need it, you should disassociate it and then release it. If an Elastic IP address is allocated but not associated with any instance, then you will be charged by AWS on an hourly basis, so if you don't have a requirement for Elastic IP addresses, it is better to release them.

VPC endpoints

A VPC endpoints is a secure way to communicate with other AWS services without using the internet, Direct Connect, VPN Connection, or a NAT device. This communication happens within the Amazon network internally so your traffic never goes out of Amazon network. At present, endpoints are supported only for **Simple Storage Service (S3)**. These endpoints are virtual devices supporting IPv4-only traffic.

An endpoint uses the private IP address of instances in your VPC to communicate with other services. You can have more than one endpoint in your VPC. You create a route in your route table for directing traffic from instance V2 in subnet 2 through your endpoint to your target service (such as S3), as shown in the following figure:

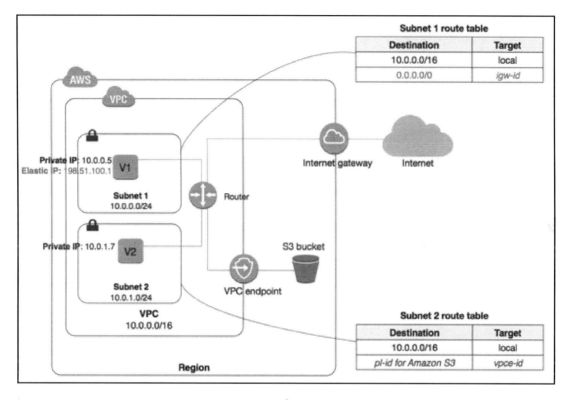

Figure 3 - AWS VPC endpoints

Network Address Translation (NAT)

You will often have resources in your VPC that will reside in private subnets that are not accessible from the internet. However, these resources will need to access the internet occasionally for patch update, software upgrade, and so on. A NAT device is used exactly for this purpose, allowing resources in private subnet to connect with either the internet or other AWS services securely. NAT devices support only IPv4 traffic.

AWS offers a NAT gateway, a managed device, and a NAT instance as NAT devices. Depending on your use case, you will choose either of them. AWS recommends a NAT gateway over a NAT instance as it is a managed service that requires little or no administration, is highly available, and highly scalable.

VPC peering

You can connect your VPC with one or more VPCs in the same region through the VPCs peering option. This connection enables you to communicate with other VPC using private IPv4 or private IPv6 addresses. Since this is a networking connection, instances in these VPCs can communicate with each other as if they are in the same network.

You can peer with VPCs in your AWS account or VPCs in other AWS accounts as well. Transitive peering is not allowed and VPCs should not have overlapping or matching IPv4 or IPv6 CIDR blocks. The following figure shows VPC peering between VPC A and VPC B. Note that the CIDR blocks differ for these two VPCs:

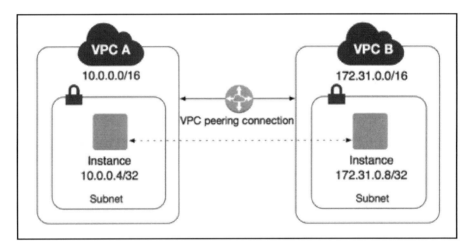

Figure 4 - AWS VPC peering

VPC features and benefits

AWS VPC offers many features and benefits to secure your resources in your own virtual network on the cloud. You can scale your resources and select resources as per your requirement in VPC just like you do in AWS, with the same level of reliability and additional security. Let's look at these features and benefits.

Multiple connectivity options

Your AWS VPC can be connected to a variety of resources, such as the internet, your on-premise data center, other VPCs in your AWS account, or VPCs in other AWS accounts; once connected, you can make your resources accessible or inaccessible in your VPC from outside of your VPC based on your requirement.

You can allow your instances in your VPC to connect with the internet directly by launching them in a subnet that is publicly accessible, also known as a public subnet. This way, your instances can send and receive traffic from the internet directly.

For instances in private subnets that are not publicly accessible, you can use a NAT device placed in a public subnet to access the internet without exposing their private IP address.

You can connect your VPC to your corporate data center by creating a secure VPN tunnel using encrypted IPsec hardware VPN connection. Once connected, all traffic between instances in your VPC and your corporate data center will be secured via this industry standard hardware VPN connection.

You can connect your VPC with other VPCs privately in the same region through the VPC peering feature. This way, you can share resources in your VPC with other virtual networks across your AWS accounts or other AWS accounts.

The VPC endpoint is used to connect to AWS services such as S3 without using internet gateway or NAT. You can also configure what users or resources are allowed to connect to these AWS services.

You can mix and match the mentioned options to support your business or application requirements. For example, you can connect VPC to your corporate data center using a hardware VPN connection, and you can allow instances in your public subnet to connect directly with the internet as well. You can configure route tables in your VPC to direct all traffic to its appropriate destination.

Secure

AWS VPC has security groups that act as an instance-level firewall and network ACLS that act as a subnet-level firewall. These advanced security features allow you to configure rules for incoming and outgoing traffic for your instances and subnets in your VPC.

With help of the VPC endpoint, you can enable access control for your data in AWS S3 so that only instances in your VPC can access that data. You can also launch dedicated instances to have isolation at the instance level; these instances have dedicated hardware for a single customer.

Simple

AWS VPC can be created using AWS Management Console in a couple of ways; you can either create it through **Start VPC Wizard**, or you can create it manually as well. You can also create VPC from AWS command-line interface.

VPC wizard gives you multiple options to create VPC, as shown in the following figure; you can pick one that suits your requirements and customize it later if needed. When you create a VPC using VPC wizard, all components of VPC, such as security groups, route tables, subnets and so on, are automatically created by VPC wizard:

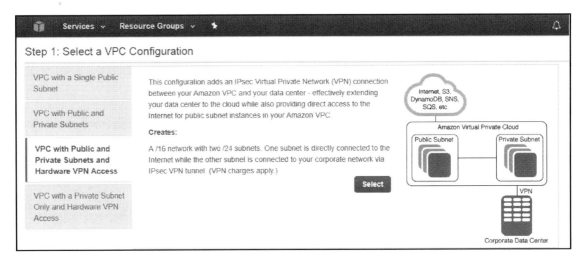

Figure 5 - AWS VPC wizard

VPC use cases

With VPC, you can control inbound and outbound access for your resources in your own virtual private network and connect your data center with AWS cloud securely along with other VPCs in your AWS accounts and VPCs in other AWS accounts. You can also securely access data on S3 from your resources in VPC without using the internet.

All these along with many other features make VPC a preferred choice for a variety of use cases, such as hosting development and testing environments in AWS VPC. You could also use VPC for creating environments for **Proof of Concept (PoC)**. These environments can be created on short notice and could act as an isolated network accessible only by specific teams or other resources. Since VPC is a software-defined network, it brings loads of flexibility in designing, integrating, and securing your resources in AWS cloud.

Let's look at some of the most popular use cases for VPC.

Hosting a public facing website

You can host a public facing website, which could be a blog, a single tier simple web application, or just a simple website using VPC. You can create a public subnet using the VPC wizard and select the **VPC with a single public subnet only** option, or you can create it manually. Secure your website using instance-level firewalls, known as security groups, allowing inbound traffic, either HTTP or HTTPS, from the internet and restricting outbound traffic to the internet when required at the same time.

Hosting multi-tier web application

Hosting a multi-tier web application requires stricter access control and more restrictions for communication between your servers for layers, such as web servers, app servers, and database servers. VPC is an ideal solution for such web applications as it has all functionalities built in.

In the following figure, there is one public subnet that contains the web server and the application server. These two instances need to have inbound and outbound access for internet traffic. This public subnet also has one NAT instance that is used to route traffic for database instance in the private subnet.

The private subnet holds instances that do not need to have access to the internet. They only need to communicate with instances in the public subnet. When an instance in the private subnet needs to access the internet for downloading patches or software update, it will do that via a NAT instance placed in the public subnet:

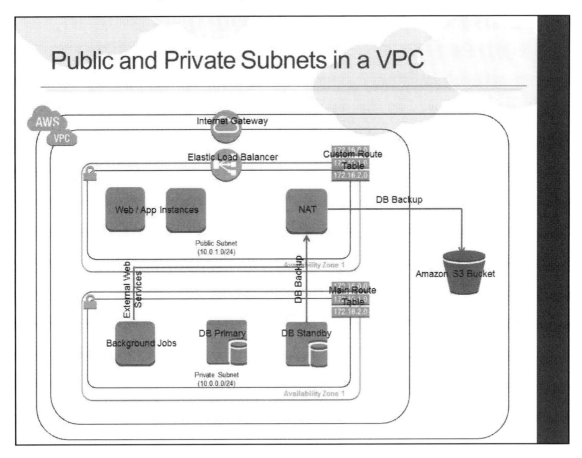

Figure 6 - AWS VPC for a multi-tier web application

Access control for this sort of architecture is configured using network ACLs that act as a firewall for subnets. You will also use security groups for configuring access at the instance level, allowing inbound and outbound access.

The VPC wizard gives you an option, **VPC with Public and Private Subnets**, to support this use case; alternatively, you can create a VPC using AWS console manually or through a command-line interface.

Creating branch office and business unit networks

Quite often, there is a requirement for connecting branch offices with their own, interconnected networks. This requirement can be fulfilled by provisioning instances within a VPC with a separate subnet for different branch offices. All resources within a VPC can communicate with each other through a private IP address by default, so all offices will be connected to each other and will also have their own local network within their own subnet.

If you need to limit communication across subnets for some instances, you can use security groups to configure access for such instances. These rules and designs can be applied to applications that are used by multiple offices within an organization. These common applications can be deployed within a VPC in a public subnet and can be configured so that they are accessible only from branch offices within an organization by configuring NACLs that acts as a firewall for subnets.

The following figure shows an example of using VPC for connecting multiple branch offices with their own local networks:

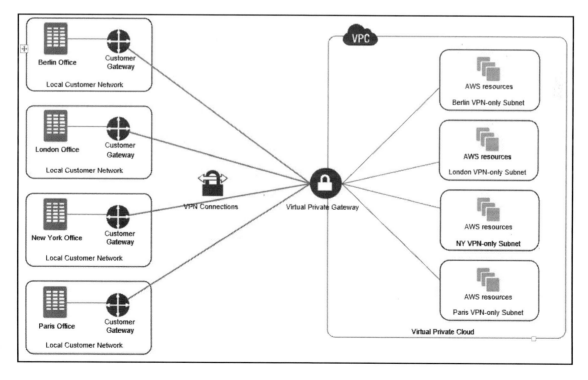

Figure 7 - AWS VPC for connecting branch offices

Hosting web applications in the AWS Cloud that are connected with your data center

Through VPC, you can also support scenarios where instances in one subnet allow inbound and outbound access to the internet and instances in other subnet can communicate exclusively with resources in your corporate data center. You will secure these communications by creating an IPsec hardware VPN connection between your VPC and your corporate network.

In this scenario, you can host your web applications in the AWS cloud in VPC and you can sync data with databases in your corporate data center through the VPN tunnel securely.

You can create a VPC for this use case using the VPC wizard and selecting **VPC with Public and Private Subnets and Hardware VPN Access**. You can also create a VPC manually through the AWS console or through the CLI.

Extending corporate network in AWS Cloud

This use case is specifically useful if you have a consistent requirement for provisioning additional resources, such as compute, storage, or database capacity to your existing infrastructure based on your workload.

This use case is also applicable to all those data centers that have reached their peak capacity and don't have room to extend further.

You can extend your corporate networking resources in the AWS cloud and take all benefits of cloud computing such as elasticity, pay-as-you-go model, security, high availability, minimal or no capex, and instant provisioning of resources by connecting your VPC with your corporate network.

You can host your VPC behind the firewall of your corporate network and ensure you move your resources to the cloud without impacting user experience or the performance of your applications. You can keep your corporate network as is and scale your resources up or down in the AWS cloud based on your requirements.

You can define your own IP address range while creating an AWS VPC, so extending your network into a VPC is similar to extending your existing corporate network in your physical data center.

To support this use case, you can create a VPC by opting for the **VPC with a Private Subnet Only and Hardware VPN Access** option in the VPC wizard or create a VPC manually. You can either connect your VPC to your data center using hardware VPN or through AWS direct connect service. The following figure shows an example of a data center extended in AWS cloud through VPC using an existing internet connection. It uses a hardware VPN connection for connecting the data center with AWS VPC:

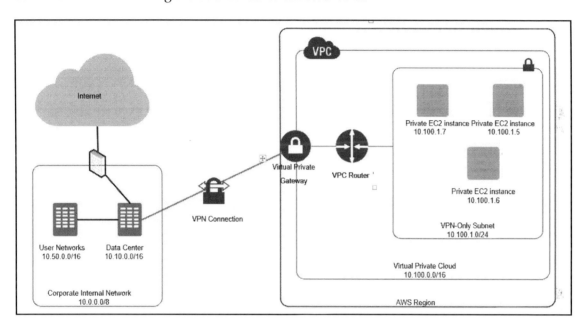

Figure 8 - AWS VPC extend corporate data center

Disaster recovery

As part of your **disaster recovery (DR)** and business continuity plan, you will need to continuously back up your critical data to your DR site. You can use a VPC to host EC2 instances with EBS volumes and store data in S3 buckets as well as in EBS volumes attached to EC2 instances securely, which can be configured to be accessible only from your network.

As part of your business continuity plan, you might want to run a small set of EC2 instances in your VPC, and these EC2 instances could be scaled quickly to meet the demand of a production workload in the event of a disaster. When the disaster is over, you could replicate data back to your data center and use servers in the data center to run your workload. Post that, you can terminate additionally provisioned resources, such as EC2 instances and RDS instances in AWS VPC.

You can plan your disaster recovery and business continuity with AWS VPC at a fraction of the cost of a traditional co-location site using physical data center. Moreover, you can automate your disaster recovery and business continuity plan using the AWS CloudFormation service; this automation will drastically reduce your deployment and provisioning time in AWS VPC when compared with a traditional physical data center.

VPC security

AWS VPC essentially carries out the task of moving IP traffic (packets) into, out of, and across AWS regions; so, the first line of defense for a VPC is to secure what traffic can enter and leave your VPC. All resources can communicate with each other within a VPC unless explicitly configured not to do that, so this leaves us primarily with securing communication outside of your VPC with resources inside your VPC and vice versa.

AWS VPC provides multiple features for securing your VPC and securing resources inside your VPC, such as security groups, network ACL, VPC Flow Logs, and controlling access for VPC. These features act as additional layers of defense while designing your VPC architecture and are used to increase security and monitor your VPC. Apart from these features, you have a routing layer available in the form of route tables.

These features enable us to implement a layered defense for an in-depth security architecture for AWS VPC that involves all layers in a network. These security features also align security controls with the application requirement of scalability, availability, and performance.

Let's look at these security features in detail.

Security groups

A security group is a virtual firewall to control ingress and egress traffic at the instance level for all instances in your VPC. Each VPC has its own default security group. When you launch an instance without assigning a security group, AWS will assign a default security group of VPC with this instance. Each instance can be assigned up to five security groups.

For a security group, in order to control ingress and egress traffic, we need to define rules for a security group. These rules need to be defined separately for controlling ingress and egress traffic. These rules are only permissive; that is, there can only be allow rules and there can't be deny rules.

When you create a new security group, by default, it does not allow any inbound traffic. You have to create a rule that allows inbound traffic. By default, a security group has a rule that allows all outbound traffic. Security groups are stateless, so if you create a rule for inbound traffic that allows traffic to flow in, this rule will allow outbound traffic as well; there is no need to create a separate rule to allow outbound traffic. These rules are editable and are applied immediately. You can add, modify, or delete a security group, and these changes are effective immediately as well. You can perform these actions from the AWS console or through the command line or an API.

An ENI can be associated with up to five security groups, while a security group can be associated with multiple instances. However, these instances cannot communicate with each other unless you configure rules in your security group to allow this. There is one exception to this behavior: the default security group already has these rules configured.

The following figure shows the security groups set up in my AWS account. This security group is created for the web server, so it has rules configured in order to allow HTTP and HTTPS traffic. It also allows SSH access on port 22 for logging into this instance:

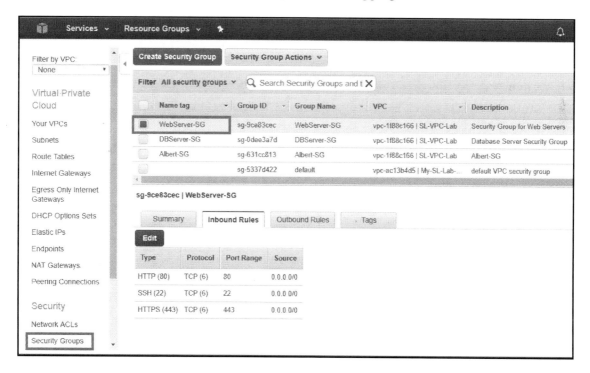

Figure 9 - AWS VPC security groups

Network access control list

The **network access control list (NACL)**, as it is popularly known, is another virtual firewall provided by AWS VPC to configure inbound and outbound traffic for your subnets inside a VPC. So, all instances within this subnet are going to use the same configuration for inbound and outbound traffic. NACLs are used for creating guardrails in an organization for your network on the cloud as it does not offer granular control. Moreover, NACLs are usually configured by system administrators in an organization.

Every VPC has a default NACL that allows all inbound and outbound traffic by default. When you create a custom NACL, it denies all inbound and outbound traffic by default. Any subnet that is not explicitly associated with an NACL is associated with a default NACL and allows all traffic, so make sure all subnets in your VPCs are explicitly associated with an NACL.

NACL uses rules similar to security groups to configure inbound and outbound traffic for a subnet. Unlike security groups, NACL gives you the option to create allow and deny rules. NACL is stateless and you will need to create separate rules for inbound and outbound traffic.

Each subnet in your VPC can be attached to only one NACL. However, one NACL can be attached to more than one subnet. Rules in NACL are evaluated from the lower to the higher number, and the highest number you can have is 32776. AWS recommends that you create rules in multiples of 100, such as 100, 200, 300, and so on, so you have room to add more rules when required.

The following figure shows network ACL for a public subnet. It allows inbound and outbound HTTP and HTTPS traffic. This NACL can be used for all public subnets that will contain all instances that need to access the internet and those that are publicly accessible:

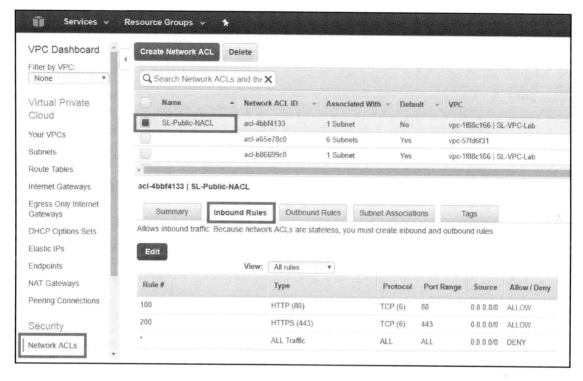

Figure 10 - AWS VPC NACL

VPC flow logs

VPC facilitates the flow of inbound and outbound traffic for all resources in your VPC. It is important to monitor the flow of this IP traffic on a continuous basis in order to ensure that all traffic is going to the desired recipient and is received from expected resources. This feature is also useful for troubleshooting issues related to traffic not reaching its destination or vice versa. The VPC flow log is a very important security tool that helps monitor the security of your network in the AWS cloud.

You can create a flow log for your VPC as well as a subnet and a network interface based on your requirement. For a VPC flow log, all resources in VPC are monitored. For a subnet flow log, all resources in a subnet are monitored. This can take up to 15 minutes to collect data after you have created a flow log.

Each network interface has a unique log stream that is published to a log group in AWS CloudWatch logs. You can create multiple flow logs publishing data to one log. These logs streams consist of flow log records that are essentially log events with fields describing all the traffic for that resource. Log streams contain flow log records, which are log events consisting of fields that describe the traffic, such as the accepted traffic or rejected traffic for that network interface.

You can configure the type of traffic you want to monitor, including accepted, rejected, or all traffic for the flow log you create. You give this log a name in CloudWatch logs, where it will be published, and choose a resource you want to monitor. You will also need the **Amazon Resource Name (ARN)** of an IAM role that will be used to publish this flow log to CloudWatch logs group. These flow logs are not real-time log streams.

You can also create flow logs for network interfaces created by other AWS services, such as AWS RDS, AWS workspaces, and so on. However, these services cannot create flow logs; instead, you should use AWS EC2 to create flow logs, either from the AWS console or through the EC2 API. VPC flow logs are offered free of charge; you are charged only for logs. You can delete a flow log if you no longer need it. It might take several minutes before this deleted flow log stops collecting data for your network interface.

VPC flow logs have certain limitations. You cannot create VPC flow logs for peered VPCs that are not in your AWS account. VPC flow logs can't be tagged. A flow log cannot be modified after it is created; you need to delete this flow log and create another one with the required configuration. Flow logs do not capture all types of traffic, such as traffic generated by instances when they contact Amazon DNS servers, traffic to and from 169.254.169.254 for getting instance metadata, and so on.

VPC access control

As discussed in IAM, all AWS services require permission to access their resources. It is imperative to define access control for VPC as well. You need to grant appropriate permissions to all users, applications, and AWS services to access all VPC resources. You can define granular, resource-level permissions for VPC, which allows you to control what resources could be accessed or modified in your VPC.

You can give permissions such as managing a VPC, a read-only permission for VPC, or managing a specific resource for VPC, such as a security group or a network ACL.

Creating VPC

Let's look at steps to create a custom VPC in an AWS account. This VPC will be created using IPv4 **Classless Inter-Domain Routing (CIDR)** block. It will have one public subnet and one public facing instance in this subnet. It will also have one private subnet and one instance in private subnet. For instance, for a private subnet to access the internet, we will use a NAT gateway in a public subnet. This VPC will have security groups and network ACL configured to allow egress and ingress internet traffic along with routes configured to support this scenario:

1. Create a VPC with a /16 IPv4 CIDR block such as 10.0.0.0/16.
2. Create an internet gateway and attach it to this VPC.
3. Create one subnet with /24 IPv4 CIDR block, such as 10.0.0.0/24, and call it a public subnet. Note that this CIDR block is a subset of a VPC CIDR block.
4. Create another subnet with /24 IPv4 CIDR block, such as 10.0.1.0/24 and call it a private subnet. Note that this CIDR block is a subset of a VPC CIDR block and it does not overlap the CIDR block of a public subnet.
5. Create a custom route table and create a route for all traffic going to the internet to go through the internet gateway. Associate this route table with the public subnet.
6. Create a NAT gateway and associate it with the public subnet. Allocate one Elastic IP address and associate it with the NAT gateway.
7. Create a custom route in the main route table for all traffic going to the internet to go through NAT gateway. Associate this route table with the private subnet. This step will facilitate the routing of all internet traffic for instances in the private subnet to go through the NAT gateway. This will ensure IP addresses for private instances are not exposed to the internet.
8. Create a network ACL for each of these subnets. Configure rules that will define inbound and outbound traffic access for these subnets. Associate these NACLs with their respective subnets.
9. Create security groups for instances to be placed in public and private subnets. Configure rules for these security groups as per the access required. Assign these security groups with instances.
10. Create one instance each in the public and private subnet for this VPC. Assign a security group to each of them. An instance in a public subnet should have either a public IP or an EIP address.
11. Verify that the public instance can access the internet and private instances can access the internet through the NAT gateway.

Once all steps are completed, our newly created custom VPC will have the following architecture. Private instances are referred to as database servers and public instances are referred to as Web servers in the diagram. Note that the NAT gateway should have the Elastic IP address to send traffic to the internet gateway as the source IP address. This VPC has both the public and private subnet in one availability zone; however, in order to have a highly available and fault-tolerant architecture, you can have a similar configuration of resources in additional availability zones:

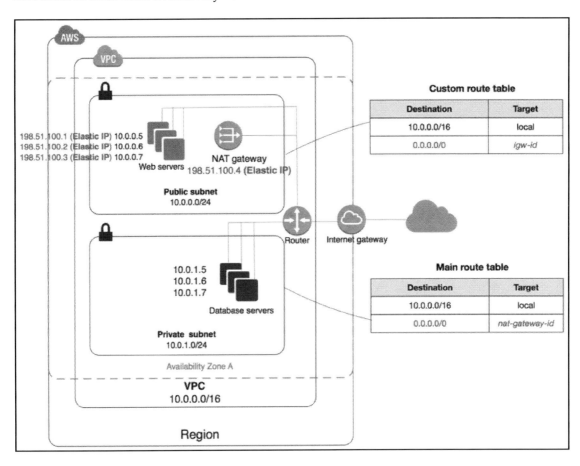

Figure 11 - AWS custom VPC

VPC connectivity options

One of the major features of AWS VPC is the connectivity options it provides for securely connecting various networks with their AWS networks. In this section, you will learn about various connectivity options for AWS VPC, such as connecting remote customer networks with VPC, connecting multiple VPCs into a shared virtual network, and so on. We will look at three connectivity options in detail:

- Connecting the user network to AWS VPC
- Connecting AWS VPC with an other AWS VPC
- Connecting the internal user with AWS VPC

Connecting user network to AWS VPC

You can extend and integrate your resources in your remote networks, such as compute power, security, monitoring, and so on, by leveraging your resources in AWS VPC. By doing this, your users can access all resources in AWS VPC seamlessly like any other resource in internal networks. This type of connectivity requires you to have non-overlapping IP ranges for your networks on the cloud and on-premises, so ensure that you have a unique CIDR block for your AWS VPC. AWS recommends that you use a unique, single, non-overlapping, and contiguous CIDR block for every VPC. You can connect your network with AWS VPC securely in the following ways:

- **Hardware VPN**: You can configure AWS-compatible customer VPN gateways to access AWS VPC over an industry standard, encrypted IPSec hardware VPN connection. You are billed for each VPN connection hour, that is, for every hour your VPC connection is up and running. Along with it, you are charged for data transfer as well.

  This option is easier to configure and install and uses an existing internet connection. It is also highly available as AWS provides two VPN tunnels in an active and standby mode by default. AWS provides virtual private gateway with two endpoints for automatic failover. You need to configure, customer gateway side of this VPN connection, this customer gateway could be software or hardware in your remote network.

  On the flip side, hardware VPN connections have data transfer speed limitation. Since they use an internet to establish connectivity, the performance of this connection, including network latency and availability, is dependent on the internet condition.

- **Direct connect**: You can connect your AWS VPC to your remote network using a dedicated network connection provided by AWS authorized partners over 1-gigabit or 10-gigabit Ethernet fiber-optic cable. One end of this cable is connected to your router, the other to an AWS Direct Connect router. You get improved, predictable network performance with reduced bandwidth cost. With direct connect, you can bypass the internet and connect directly to your resources in AWS, including AWS VPC.

  You can pair direct connect with a hardware VPN connection for a redundant, highly available connectivity between your remote networks and AWS VPC. The following diagram shows the AWS direct connect service interfacing with your remote network:

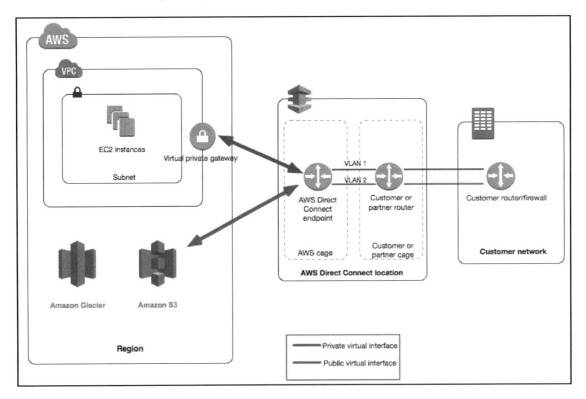

Figure 12 - AWS direct connect

- **AWS VPN CloudHub**: You might have multiple remote networks that need to connect securely with AWS VPC. For such scenarios, you will create multiple VPN connections, and you will use AWS VPN CloudHub to provide secure communication between these sites. This is a hub and spoke model that can be used either for primary connectivity or as a backup option. It uses existing internet connections and VPN connections.

  You create a virtual private gateway for your VPC with multiple customer gateways for your remote networks to use AWS VPN CloudHub. These remote networks should not have overlapping IP networks. The pricing model for this option is similar to that of a hardware VPN connection.

- **Software VPN**: Instead of a hardware VPN connection, you can also use an EC2 instance in your VPC with a software VPN appliance running in order to connect your remote network. AWS does not provide any software VPN appliance; however, you can use software VPN appliances through a range of products provided by AWS partners and various open source communities present on AWS marketplace. It also uses the internet for connectivity; hence, reliability, availability, and network performance are dependent on the internet speed.

  This option, however, supports a wide variety of VPN vendors, products, and protocols. It is completely managed by customers. It is helpful for scenarios where you are required to manage both ends of a connection, either for compliance purposes or if you are using connectivity devices that are currently not supported by AWS.

Connecting AWS VPC with other AWS VPC

If you have multiple VPCs in multiple regions across the globe, you may want to connect these VPCs to create a larger, secure network. This connectivity option works only if your VPCs do not have overlapping IP ranges and have a unique CIDR block. Let's look at the following ways to connect AWS VPC with other AWS VPCs:

VPC peering: You can connect two VPCs in the same region using a VPC peering option in AWS VPC. Resources in these VPCs can communicate with each other using private IP addresses as if they are in the same network. You can have a VPC peering connection with a VPC in your AWS account and VPC in other AWS accounts as long as they are in the same region.

AWS uses its own existing infrastructure for this connection. It is not a gateway or a VPN connection that uses any physical device. It is not a single point of failure or a network performance bottleneck.

VPC peering is the most preferred method of connecting AWS VPCs. It is suited for many scenarios for large and small organizations. Let's look at some of the most common scenarios.

If you need to provide full access to resources across two or more VPCs, you can do that by peering them. For example, you have multiple branch offices in various regions across the globe and each branch office has a different VPC. Your headquarter needs to access all resources for all VPCs for all your branch offices. You can accomplish this by creating a VPC in each region and peering all other VPCs with your VPC.

You might have a centralized VPC that contains information required by other VPCs in your organization, such as policies related to human resources. This is a read-only VPC and you would not want to provide full access to resources in this VPC. You can create VPC peering connection and restrict access for this centralized VPC.

You can also have a centralized VPC that might be shared with your customers. Each customer can peer their VPC with your centralized VPC, but they cannot access resources in other customers' VPC.

Data transfer charges for a VPC peering connection are similar to charges for data transfer across availability zones. As discussed, VPC peering is limited to VPCs in the same region. A VPC peering is a one-to-one connection between two VPCs; transitive peering is not allowed for a peering connection. In the following diagram, VPC A is peered with VPC B and VPC C; however, VPC B is not peered with VPC C implicitly. It has to be peered explicitly:

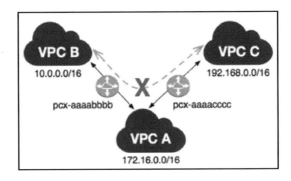

Figure 13 - AWS VPC Transitive Peering

Apart from VPC peering, there are other options for connecting VPCs, such as software VPN, hardware VPN, and AWS direct connect as well. All of these options have benefits and limitations similar to the one discussed in the previous section.

Connecting internal user with AWS VPC

If you want to allow your internal users to access resources in AWS VPC, you can leverage your existing remote networks to AWS VPC connections using either hardware VPN, direct connect, or software VPN depending on your requirement. Alternatively, you can combine these connectivity options to suit your requirements, such as cost, speed, reliability, availability, and so on.

VPC limits

AWS VPC has limits for various components in a region. Most of these are soft limits and can be increased by contacting AWS support from the AWS console and submitting a request by filling the Amazon VPC limits form available in the AWS console.

Let's look at these limits:

Resource	Default limit
VPCs per region	5
Subnets per VPC	200
Elastic IP addresses per region	5
Flow logs per resource in a region	2
Customer gateways per region	50
Internet gateways per region	5
NAT gateways per availability zone	5
Virtual private gateways per region	5
Network ACLs per VPC	200
Rules per network ACL	20
Network interfaces per region	350
Route tables per VPC	200
Routes per route table	50
Security groups per VPC (per region)	500
Rules per security group	50

Security groups per network interface	5
Active VPC peering connections per VPC	50
VPC endpoints per region	20
VPN connections per region	50
VPN connections per VPC (per virtual private gateway)	10

Table 1 - AWS VPC limit

VPC best practices

In this section, we will go through an exhaustive list of best practices to be followed for AWS VPC. Most of these are recommended by AWS as well. Implementing these best practices will ensure that your resources, including your servers, data, and applications, are integrated with other AWS services and secured in AWS VPC. Remember that VPC is not a typical data center and it should not be treated as one.

Plan your VPC before you create it

Always start by planning and designing architecture for your VPC before you create it. A bad VPC design will have serious implications on the flexibility, scalability, availability, and security of your infrastructure. So, spend a good amount of time planning out your VPC before you actually start creating it.

Start with the objective of creating a VPC: is it for one application or for a business unit? Spec out all subnets you will need and figure out your availability and fault- tolerance requirements. Find out what all connectivity options you will need for connecting all internal and external networks. You might need to plan for a number of VPCs if you need to connect with networks in more than one region.

Choose the highest CIDR block

Once you create VPC with a CIDR block, you cannot change it. You will have to create another VPC and migrate your resources to a new VPC if you want to change your CIDR block. So, take a good look at your current resources and your requirements for the next few years in order to plan and design your VPC architecture. A VPC can have a CIDR block ranging from /16 to /28, which means you can have between 65,536 and 16 IP addresses for your VPC. AWS recommends that you choose the highest CIDR block available, so always go for /16 CIDR block for your VPC. This way, you won't be short of IP addresses if you need to increase your instances exponentially.

Unique IP address range

All VPC connectivity options require you to have non-overlapping IP ranges. Consider future connectivity to all your internal and external networks. Make sure you take note of all available IP ranges for all your environments, including remote networks, data centers, offices, other AWS VPCs, and so on, before you assign CIDR ranges for your VPC. None of these should conflict and overlap with any network that you want to connect with.

Leave the default VPC alone

AWS provides a default VPC in every region for your AWS account. It is best to leave this VPC alone and start with a custom VPC for your requirement. The default VPC has all components associated with it; however, the security configuration of all these components, such as subnets, security groups, and network ACLs are quite open to the world. There is no private subnet either. So, it is a good idea to create your own VPC from scratch using either a VPC wizard in the AWS console or creating it manually through the AWS console or AWS CLI. You can configure all resources as per your requirement for your custom VPC.

Moreover, by default, if a subnet is not associated with a route table or an NACL, it is associated with the main route table and default NACL. These two components don't have any restrictions on inbound and outbound traffic, and you risk exposing your resources to the entire world.

You should not modify the main route table either; doing that might give other subnets routes that they shouldn't be given. Always create a custom route table and keep the main route table as it is.

Design for region expansion

AWS keeps on expanding its regions by adding more availability zones to them. We know that one subnet cannot span more than one availability zone, and distributing our resources across availability zones makes our application highly available and fault-tolerant. It is a good idea to reserve some IP address for future expansion while creating subnets with a subset of VPC CIDR block. By default, AWS reserves five IP address in every subnet for internal usage; make a note of this while allocating IP addresses to a subnet.

Tier your subnets

Ideally, you should design your subnets according to your architecture tiers, such as the database tier, the application tier, the business tier, and so on, based on their routing needs, such as public subnets needing a route to the internet gateway, and so on. You should also create multiple subnets in as many availability zones as possible to improve your fault-tolerance. Each availability zone should have identically sized subnets, and each of these subnets should use a routing table designed for them depending on their routing need. Distribute your address space evenly across availability zones and keep the reserved space for future expansion.

Follow the least privilege principle

For every resource you provision or configure in your VPC, follow the least privilege principle. So, if a subnet has resources that do not need to access the internet, it should be a private subnet and should have routing based on this requirement. Similarly, security groups and NACLs should have rules based on this principle. They should allow access only for traffic required. Do not add a route to the internet gateway to the main route table as it is the default route table for all subnets.

Keep most resources in the private subnet

In order to keep your VPC and resources in your VPC secure, ensure that most of the resources are inside a private subnet by default. If you have instances that need to communicate with the internet, then you should add an **Elastic Load Balancer** (**ELB**) in the public subnet and add all instances behind this ELB in the private subnet.

Use NAT devices (a NAT instance or a NAT gateway) to access public networks from your private subnet. AWS recommends that you use a NAT gateway over a NAT instance as the NAT gateway is a fully managed, highly available, and redundant component.

Creating VPCs for different use cases

You should ideally create one VPC each for your development, testing, and production environments. This will secure your resources from keeping them separate from each other, and it will also reduce your blast radius, that is, the impact on your environment if one of your VPCs goes down.

For most use cases such as application isolation, multi-tenant application, and business unit alignment, it is a good idea to create a separate VPC.

Favor security groups over NACLs

Security groups and NACLs are virtual firewalls available for configuring security rules for your instances and subnets respectively. While security groups are easier to configure and manage, NACLs are different. It is recommended that NACLs be used sparingly and not be changed often. NACLs should be the security policy for your organization as it does not work at a granular level. NACL rules are tied to the IP address and for a subnet, with the addition of every single rule, the complexity and management of these rules becomes exponentially difficult.

Security group rules are tied to instances and these rules span the entire VPC; they are stateful and dynamic in nature. They are easier to manage and should be kept simple. Moreover, security groups can pass other security groups as an object reference in order to allow access, so you can allow access to your database server security group only for the application server security group.

IAM your VPC

Access control for your VPC should be on top of your list while creating a VPC. You can configure IAM roles for your instances and assign them at any point. You can provide granular access for provisioning new resources inside a VPC and reduce the blast radius by restricting access to high-impact components such as various connectivity options, NACL configuration, subnet creation, and so on.

There will usually be more than one person managing all resources for your VPC; you should assign permissions to these people based on their role and by following the principle of least privileges. If someone does not need access to a resource, that access shouldn't be given in the first place.

Periodically, use the access advisor function available in IAM to find out whether all the permissions are being used as expected and take necessary actions based on your findings.

Create an IAM VPC admin group to manage your VPC and its resources.

Using VPC peering

Use VPC peering whenever possible. When you connect two VPCs using the VPC peering option, instances in these VPCs can communicate with each other using a private IP address. For a VPC peering connection, AWS uses its own network and you do not have to rely on an external network for the performance of your connection, and it is a lot more secure.

Using Elastic IP instead of public IP

Always use **Elastic IP (EIP)** instead of public IP for all resources that need to connect to the internet. The EIPs are associated with an AWS account instead of an instance. They can be assigned to an instance in any state, whether the instance is running or whether it is stopped. It persists without an instance so you can have high availability for your application depending on an IP address. The EIP can be reassigned and moved to **Elastic Network Interface (ENI)** as well. Since these IPs don't change, they can be whitelisted by target resources.

All these advantages of EIP over a public IP make it more favorable when compared with a public IP.

Tagging in VPC

Always tag your resources in a VPC. The tagging strategy should be part of your planning phase. A good practice is to tag a resource immediately after it is created. Some common tags include version, owner, team, project code, cost center, and so on. Tags are supported by AWS billing and for resource-level permissions.

Monitoring a VPC

Monitoring is imperative to the security of any network, such as AWS VPC. Enable AWS CloudTrail and VPC flow logs to monitor all activities and traffic movement. The AWS CloudTrail will record all activities, such as provisioning, configuring, and modifying all VPC components. The VPC flow log will record all the data flowing in and out of the VPC for all the resources in VPC. Additionally, you can set up config rules for the AWS Config service for your VPC for all resources that should not have changes in their configuration.

Connect these logs and rules with AWS CloudWatch to notify you of anything that is not expected behavior and control changes within your VPC. Identify irregularities within your network, such as resources receiving unexpected traffic in your VPC, adding instances in the VPC with configuration not approved by your organization, among others.

Similarly, if you have unused resources lying in your VPC, such as security groups, EIP, gateways, and so on, remove them by automating the monitoring of these resources.

Lastly, you can use third-party solutions available on AWS marketplace for monitoring your VPC. These solutions integrate with existing AWS monitoring solutions, such as AWS CloudWatch, AWS CloudTrail, and so on, and provide information in a user-friendly way in the form of dashboards.

Summary

The VPC is responsible for securing your network, including your infrastructure on the cloud, and that makes this AWS service extremely critical for mastering security in AWS. In this chapter, you learned the basics of VPC, including features, benefits, and most common use cases.

We went through the various components of VPC and you learned how to configure all of them to create a custom VPC. Alongside, we looked at components that make VPC secure, such as routing, security groups, and so on.

We also looked at multiple connectivity options, such as a private, shared, or dedicated connection provided by VPC. These connectivity options enable us to create a hybrid cloud environment, a large connected internal network for your organization, and many such secure, highly available environments to address many more scenarios.

Lastly, you learned about the limits of various VPC components and we looked at an exhaustive list of VPC best practices.

In the next chapter, we will look at ways to secure data in AWS: data security in AWS in a nutshell. You will learn about encrypting data in transit and at rest. We will also look at securing data using various AWS services.

4

Data Security in AWS

Data security in the AWS platform can be classified into two broad categories:

- Protecting data at rest
- Protecting data in transit

Furthermore, data security has the following components that help in securing data in multiple ways:

- Data encryption
- **Key Management Services (KMS)**
- Access control
- AWS service security features

AWS provides you with various tools and services to secure your data in AWS when your data is in transit or when your data is at rest. These tools and services include resource access control using AWS **Identity and Access Management (IAM)**, data encryption, and managed KMS, such as AWS KMS for creating and controlling keys used for data encryption. The AWS KMS provides multiple options for managing your entire **Key Management Infrastructure (KMI)**. Alternatively, you also have the option to go with the fully managed AWS CloudHSM service, a cloud-based **hardware security module (HSM)** that helps you generate and use your own keys for encryption purpose.

AWS recently launched a new security service to protect your sensitive data by using machine learning algorithms; this service is called Amazon Macie. As of now, it offers security for all data stored in your Amazon **Simple Storage Service (S3)**.

If you want to protect your data further due to business or regulatory compliance purposes, you can enable additional features for accidental deletion of data such as the versioning feature in AWS S3, MFA for accessing and deleting data, enable cross-region replication for more than one copy of your data in AWS S3, and so on.

All data storage and data processing AWS services provide multiple features to secure your data. Such features include data encryption at rest, data encryption in transit, MFA for access control and for deletion of data, versioning for accidental data deletion, granular access control and authorization policies, cross-region replication, and so on.

Chapter overview

In this chapter, we will learn about protecting data in the AWS platform for various AWS services. To begin with, we will go over the fundamentals of encryption and decryption and how encryption and decryption of data work in AWS. Post that, we will start with security features for securing data in transit and at rest for each of the following AWS services:

- Amazon **Simple Storage Service (S3)**
- Amazon **Elastic Block Storage (EBS)**
- Amazon **Relational Database Service (RDS)**
- Amazon Glacier
- Amazon DynamoDB
- Amazon **Elastic Map Reduce (EMR)**

We will look at data encryption in AWS and we will learn about three models that are available for managing keys for encryption and how we can use these models for encrypting data in various AWS services such as, AWS S3, Amazon EBS, AWS Storage Gateway, Amazon RDS, and so on.

Next, we will deep dive on AWS KMS and go through KMS features and major KMS components.

Furthermore, we will go through the AWS CloudHSM service with its benefits and popular use cases.

Lastly, we will take a look at Amazon Macie, the newest security service launched by AWS to protect sensitive data using machine learning at the backend.

Encryption and decryption fundamentals

Encryption of data can be defined as converting data known as plaintext into code, often known as ciphertext, that is unreadable by anyone except the intended audience. Data encryption is the most popular way of adding another layer of security for preventing unauthorized access and use of data. Encryption is a two-step process: in the first step, data is encrypted using a combination of an encryption key and an encryption algorithm, in the second step, data is decrypted using a combination of a decryption key and a decryption algorithm to view data in its original form.

The following three components are required for encryption. These three components work hand in hand for securing your data:

- Data to be encrypted
- Algorithm for encryption
- Encryption keys to be used alongside the data and the algorithm

There are two types of encryption available, symmetric and asymmetric. Asymmetric encryption is also known as public key encryption. Symmetric encryption uses the same secret key to perform both the encryption and decryption processes. On the other hand, asymmetric encryption uses two keys, a public key for encryption and a corresponding private key for decryption, making this option more secure and at the same time more difficult to maintain as you would need to manage two separate keys for encryption and decryption.

 AWS only uses symmetric encryption

For encrypting data in AWS, the plaintext data key is used to convert plaintext data into ciphertext using the encryption algorithm. The following figure shows a typical workflow of the data encryption process in AWS:

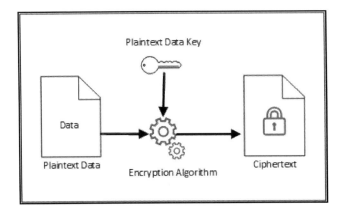

Figure 1 - AWS encryption workflow

Decryption converts the encrypted data (ciphertext) into plaintext, essentially reversing the encryption process. For decrypting data in AWS, ciphertext uses the plaintext data key for converting ciphertext into plaintext by applying the decryption algorithm. The following figure shows the AWS decryption workflow for converting ciphertext into plaintext:

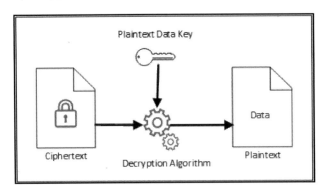

Figure 2 - AWS decryption workflow

Envelope encryption

AWS uses envelope encryption, a process to encrypt data directly. This process provides a balance between the process and security for encrypting your data. This process has the following steps for encrypting and storing your data:

1. The AWS service being used for encryption will generate a data key when a user requests data to be encrypted.
2. This data key is used to encrypt data along with the encryption algorithm.
3. Once the data is encrypted, the data key is encrypted as well by using the key-encrypting key that is unique to the AWS service used to store your data such, as AWS S3.
4. This encrypted data and encrypted data key are stored in the AWS storage service.

Note that the key-encrypting key also known as master key is stored and managed separately from the data and the data key itself. When decrypted data is required to be converted to plaintext data, the preceding mentioned process is reversed.

The following figure depicts the end-to-end workflow for the envelope encryption process; the master key in the following figure is the key-encrypting key:

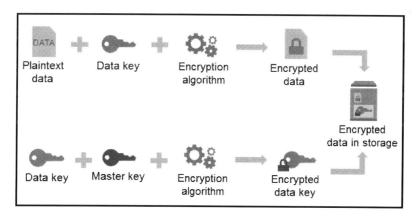

Figure 3 - AWS envelope encryption

Securing data at rest

You might be required to encrypt your data at rest for all AWS services or for some of the AWS storage services depending on your organizational policies, industry or government regulations, compliance, or simply for adding another layer of security for your data. AWS provides several options for encrypting data at rest including fully automated and fully managed AWS encryption solutions, manual encryption solutions, client-side encryption, and so on. In this section, we are going to go over these options for each AWS storage service.

Amazon S3

The S3 is one of the major and most commonly used storage services in the AWS platform. It supports a wide range of use cases such as file storage, archival records, disaster recovery, website hosting, and so on. The S3 provides multiple features to protect your data such as encryption, MFA, versioning, access control policies, cross-region replication, and so on. Let us look at these features for protecting your data at rest in S3:

Permissions

The S3 gives you an option to add bucket level and object level permissions in addition to the IAM policies for better access control. These permissions allow you to control information theft, data integrity, unauthorized access, and deletion of your data.

Versioning

The S3 has a versioning feature that maintains all versions of objects that are modified or deleted in a bucket. Versioning prevents accidental deletion and overwrites for all your objects. You can restore an object to its previous version if it is compromised. Versioning is disabled by default. Once versioning is enabled for a bucket, it can only be suspended. It cannot be disabled.

Replication

In order to provide the 11 9s of durability (99.999999999), S3 replicates each object stored across all availability zones within the respective region. This process ensures data availability in the event of a disaster by maintaining multiple copies of your data within a region. The S3 also offers a cross region replication feature that is used to automatically and asynchronously replicate objects stored in your bucket from one region to an S3 bucket in another region. This bucket level feature can be used to backup your s3 objects across regions.

Server-Side encryption

The S3 provides server-side encryption feature for encrypting user data. This encryption process is transparent to the end user (client) as it is performed at the server side. AWS manages the master key used for this encryption and ensures that this key is rotated on a regular basis. AWS generates a unique encryption key for each object and then encrypts the object using AES-256. The encryption key then encrypts itself using AES-256, with a master key that is stored in a secure location.

Client-Side encryption

The AWS also supports client-side encryption where encryption keys are created and managed by you. Data is encrypted by your applications before it is submitted to AWS for storage and the data is decrypted after it is received from the AWS services. The data is stored in the AWS service in an encrypted form and AWS has no knowledge of encryption algorithms or keys used to encrypt this data. You can also use either symmetric or asymmetric keys along with any encryption algorithm for client-side encryption. AWS provided Java SDK, offers client-side encryption features for Amazon S3.

Amazon EBS

Amazon EBS is an abstract block storage service providing persistent block level storage volumes. These volumes are attached to Amazon **Elastic Compute Cloud (EC2)** instances. Each of these volumes is automatically replicated within its availability zone that protects against component failure of an EBS volume. Let us look at options available to protect data at rest, stored in EBS volumes that are attached to an EC2 instance.

Replication

AWS stores each EBS volume as a file and creates two copies of this volume in the same availability zone. This replication process provides redundancy against hardware failure. However, for the purpose of disaster recovery, AWS recommends replicating data at the application level.

Backup

You can create snapshots for your EBS volumes to get point in time copies of your data stored in EBS volume. These snapshots are stored in AWS S3 so they provide the same durability as any other object stored in S3. If an EBS volume is corrupt or if data is modified or deleted from an EBS volume, you can use snapshots to restore the data to its desired state. You can authorize access for these snapshots through IAM as well. These EBS snapshots are AWS objects to which you can assign permissions for your IAM identities such as users, groups, and roles.

Encryption

You can encrypt data in your EBS volumes using AWS native encryption features such as AWS KMS. When you create an snapshot of an encrypted volume, you get an encrypted snapshot. You can use these encrypted EBS volume to store your data securely at rest and attach these to your EC2 instances.

The **Input Output Per Second (IOPS)** performance of an encrypted volume is similar to an unencrypted volume, with negligible effect on latency. Moreover, an encrypted volume can be accessed in a similar way as an unencrypted volume. One of the best parts about encrypting EBS volume is that both encryption and decryption require no additional action from the user, EC2 instance, or the user's application, and they are handled transparently.

Snapshots of encrypted volumes are automatically encrypted. Volumes created using these encrypted snapshots are also automatically encrypted.

Amazon RDS

Amazon RDS enables you to encrypt your data for EBS volumes, snapshots, read replicas and automated backups of your RDS instances. One of the benefits of working with RDS is that you do not have to write any decryption algorithm to decrypt your encrypted data stored in RDS. This process of decryption is handled by Amazon RDS.

Amazon Glacier

AWS uses AES-256 for encrypting each Amazon Glacier archive and generates separate unique encryption keys for each of these archives. By default, all data stored on Amazon Glacier is protected using the server-side encryption. The encryption key is then encrypted itself by using the AES-256 with a master key. This master key is rotated regularly and stored in a secure location.

Additionally, you can encrypt data prior to uploading it to the Amazon Glacier if you want more security for your data at rest.

Amazon DynamoDB

Amazon DynamoDB can be used without adding protection. However, for additional protection, you can also implement a data encryption layer over the standard DynamoDB service. DynamoDB supports number, string, and raw binary data type formats. When storing encrypted fields in DynamoDB, it is a best practice to use raw binary fields or Base64-encoded string fields.

Amazon EMR

Amazon EMR is a managed Hadoop Framework service in the cloud. AWS provides the AMIs for Amazon EMR, and you can't use custom AMIs or your own EBS volumes.

Amazon EMR automatically configures Amazon EC2 firewall settings such as network **access control list (ACL)** and security groups for controlling network access for instances. These EMR clusters are launched in an Amazon **Virtual Private Cloud (VPC)**.

By default, Amazon EMR instances do not encrypt data at rest. Usually, EMR clusters store data in S3 or in DynamoDB for persistent data. This data can be secured using the security options for these Amazon services as mentioned in the earlier sections.

Securing data in transit

Most of the web applications that are hosted on AWS will be sending data over the internet and it is imperative to protect data in transit. This transit will involve network traffic between clients and servers, and network traffic between servers. So data in transit needs to be protected at the network layer and the session layer.

AWS services provide IPSec and SSL/TLS support for securing data in transit. An IPSec protocol extends the IP protocol stack primarily for the network layer and allows applications on the upper layers to communicate securely without modification. The SSL/TLS, however, operates at the session layer.

The **Transport Layer Security (TLS)** is a standard set of protocols for securing communications over a network. TLS has evolved from **Secure Sockets Layer (SSL)** and is considered to be a more refined system.

Let us look at options to secure network traffic in AWS for various AWS services.

Amazon S3

The AWS S3 supports the SSL/TLS protocol for encrypting data in transit by default. All data requests in AWS S3 is accessed using HTTPS. This includes AWS S3 service management requests such as saving an object to an S3 bucket, user payload such as content and the metadata of objects saved, modified, or fetched from S3 buckets.

You can access S3 using either the AWS Management Console or through S3 APIs.

When you access S3 through AWS Management Console, a secure SSL/TLS connection is established between the service console endpoint and the client browser. This connection secures all subsequent traffic for this session.

When you access S3 through S3 APIs that is through programs, an SSL/TLS connection is established between the AWS S3 endpoint and client. This secure connection then encapsulates all requests and responses within this session.

Amazon RDS

You have an option to connect to the AWS RDS service through your AWS EC2 instance within the same region. If you use this option, you can use the existing security of the AWS network and rely on it. However, if you are connecting to AWS RDS using the internet, you'll need additional protection in the form of TLS/SSL.

As of now SSL/TLS is currently supported by AWS RDS MySQL and Microsoft SQL instance connections only.

AWS RDS for Oracle native network encryption encrypts the data in transit. It helps you to encrypt network traffic traveling over Oracle Net services.

Amazon DynamoDB

You can connect to AWS DynamoDB using other AWS services in the same region and while doing so, you can use the existing security of AWS network and rely on it. However, while accessing AWS DynamoDB from the internet, you might want to use HTTP over SSL/TLS (HTTPS) for enhanced security. AWS advises users to avoid HTTP access for all connections over the internet for AWS DynamoDB and other AWS services.

Amazon EMR

Amazon EMR offers several encryption options for securing data in transit. These options are open source features, application specific, and vary by EMR version.

For traffic between Hadoop nodes, no additional security is usually required as all nodes reside in the same availability zone for Amazon EMR. These nodes are secured by the AWS standard security measures at the physical and infrastructure layer.

For traffic between Hadoop cluster and Amazon S3, Amazon EMR uses HTTPS for sending data between EC2 and S3. It uses HTTPS by default for sending data between the Hadoop cluster and the Amazon DynamoDB as well.

For traffic between users or applications interacting with the Hadoop cluster, it is advisable to use SSH or REST protocols for interactive access to applications. You can also use Thrift or Avro protocols along with SSL/TLS.

For managing a Hadoop cluster, you would need to access the EMR master node. You should use SSH to access the EMR master node for administrative tasks and for managing the Hadoop cluster.

AWS KMS

AWS KMS is a fully managed service that supports encryption for your data at rest and data in transit while working with AWS services. AWS KMS lets you create and manage keys that are used to encrypt your data. It provides a fully managed and highly available key storage, management and auditing solution that can be used to encrypt data across AWS services as well as to encrypt data within your applications. It is low cost as default keys are stored in your account at no charge – you pay for key usage and for creating any additional master keys.

KMS benefits

AWS KMS has various benefits such as importing your own keys in KMS and creating keys with aliases and description. You can disable keys temporarily and re-enable them. You can also delete keys that are no longer required or used. You can rotate your keys periodically or let AWS rotate them annually. Let us look at some major benefits of KMS in detail:

Fully managed

AWS KMS is a fully managed service, where AWS takes care of underlying infrastructure to support high availability as it is deployed in multiple availability zones within a region, automatic scalability, security, and zero maintenance for the user. This allows the user to focus on the encryption requirement for their workload. AWS KMS provides 99.999999999% durability for your encrypted keys by storing multiple copies of these keys.

Centralized Key Management

AWS KMS gives you centralized control of all of your encryption keys. You can access KMS through the AWS Management Console, CLI, and AWS SDK for creating, importing, and rotating keys. You can also set up usage policies and audit KMS for key usage from any of these options for accessing AWS KMS.

Integration with AWS services

AWS KMS integrates seamlessly with multiple AWS services to enable encryption of data stored in these AWS services such as S3, RDS, EMR, and so on. AWS KMS also integrates with management services, such as AWS CloudTrail, to log usage of each key, every single time it is used for audit purpose. It also integrates with IAM to provide access control.

Secure and compliant

The AWS KMS is a secure service that ensures your master keys are not shared with anyone else. It uses hardened systems and hardening techniques to protect your unencrypted master keys. KMS keys are never transmitted outside of the AWS regions in which they were created. You can define which users can use keys and have granular permissions for accessing KMS.

The AWS KMS is compliant with many leading regulatory compliance schemes such as PCI-DSS Level 1, SOC1, SOC2, SOC3, ISO 9001, and so on.

KMS components

Let us look at the important components of AWS KMS and understand how they work together to secure data in AWS. The envelope encryption is one of the key components of KMS that we discussed earlier in this chapter.

Customer master key (CMK)

The CMK is a primary component of KMS. These keys could be managed either by the customer or by AWS. You would usually need CMKs to protect your data keys (keys used for encrypting data). Each of these keys can be used to protect 4 KB of data directly. These CMKs are always encrypted when they leave AWS. For every AWS service that integrates with AWS KMS, AWS provides a CMK that is managed by AWS. This CMK is unique to your AWS account and region in which it is used.

Data keys

Data keys are used to encrypt data. This data could be in your application outside of AWS. AWS KMS can be used to generate, encrypt, and decrypt data keys. However, AWS KMS does not store, manage, or track your data keys. These functions should be performed by you in your application.

Key policies

A key policy is a document that contains permission for accessing CMK. You can decide who can use and manage CMK for all CMK that you create, and you can add this information to the key policy. This key policy can be edited to add, modify, or delete permissions for a customer managed CMK; however, a key policy for an AWS managed CMK cannot be edited.

Auditing CMK usage

AWS KMS integrates with AWS CloudTrail to provide an audit trail of your key usage. You can save this trail that is generated as a log file in a S3 bucket. These log files contain information about all AWS KMS API requests made in the AWS Management Console, AWS SDKs, command line tools such as AWS CLI and all requests made through other AWS services that are integrated with AWS KMS. These log files will tell you about KMS operation, the identity of a requester along with the IP address, time of usage, and so on.

You can monitor, control, and investigate your key usage through AWS CloudTrail.

Key Management Infrastructure (KMI)

AWS KMS provides a secure KMI as a service to you. While encrypting and decrypting data, it is the responsibility of the KMI provider to keep your keys secure, and AWS KMS helps you keep your keys secure. The KMS is a managed service so you don't have to worry about scaling your infrastructure when your encryption requirement is increasing.

AWS CloudHSM

AWS and AWS partners offer various options such as AWS KMS to protect your data in AWS. However, due to contractual, regulatory compliance, or corporate requirements for security of an application or sensitive data, you might need additional protection. AWS CloudHSM is a cloud-based dedicated, single-tenant HSM allowing you to include secure key storage and high-performance crypto operations to your applications on the AWS platform. It enables you to securely generate, store, manage, and protect encryption keys in a way that these keys are accessible only by you or authorized users that only you specify and no one else.

AWS CloudHSM is a fully managed service that takes care of administrative, time-consuming tasks such as backups, software updates, hardware provisioning, and high availability by automating these tasks. However, AWS does not have any access to configure, create, manage, or use your CloudHSM. You can quickly scale by adding or removing HSM capacity on-demand with no upfront costs.

An HSM is a hardware device providing secure key storage and cryptographic operations inside a tamper-proof hardware appliance.

AWS CloudHSM runs in your VPC, as shown in the following figure, so it is secure by design as all VPC security features are available to secure your CloudHSM:

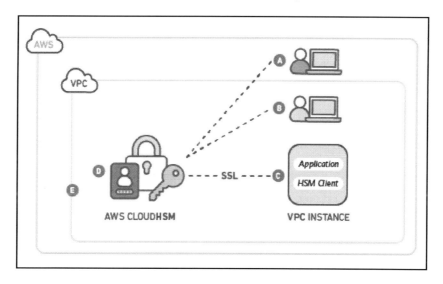

Figure 4 - AWS CloudHSM

CloudHSM features

Let us look at some features of the AWS CloudHSM service:

Generate and use encryption keys using HSMs

AWS CloudHSM provides FIPS 140-2 level 3 compliant HSM for using and generating your encryption keys. It protects your encryption keys with a single tenant, exclusive access, and dedicated tamper-proof device in your own AWS VPC.

Pay as you go model

AWS CloudHSM offers a utility pricing model like many other AWS services. You pay only for what you use and there are no upfront costs whatsoever. You are billed for every running hour (or partial hour) for every HSM you provision within a CloudHSM cluster.

Easy To manage

AWS CloudHSM is a fully managed service, so you need not worry about scalability, high availability, hardware provisioning, or software patching. These tasks are taken care by of AWS. The AWS also takes automated encrypted backups of your HSM on a daily basis.

AWS monitors health and network availability of HSMs. It does not have access to keys stored inside these HSMs. This access is available only to you and users authorized by you. You are responsible for keys and cryptography operations. This separation of duties and role-based access control is inherent to CloudHSM design, as shown in the following figure:

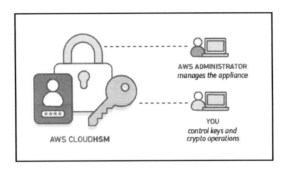

Figure 5 - AWS CloudHSM separation of duties

AWS CloudHSM use cases

A CloudHSM cluster can store up to 3,500 keys of any type or size. It integrates with AWS CloudTrail so all activities related to CloudHSM are logged and you can get a history of all AWS API calls made to CloudHSM.

With so many features and benefits, AWS CloudHSM has many use cases when it comes to securing your data. Let us look at some of the most popular use cases for this service:

Offload SSL/TLS processing for web servers

Web servers and web browsers often use SSL or TLS for a secure connection to transfer data over the internet. This connection requires the web server to use a public-private key pair along with a public key certificate in order to establish an HTTPS session with each client. This activity acts as an overhead for the web server in terms of additional computation. CloudHSM can help you offload this overhead by storing the web server's private key in HSM as it is designed for this purpose. This process is often known as SSL acceleration.

Protect private keys for an issuing certificate authority

A certificate authority is an entity entrusted for issuing digital certificates for a public key infrastructure. These digital certificates are used by an individual or an organization for various scenarios by binding public keys to an identity. You need to protect private keys that are used to sign the certificates used by your certificate authority. CloudHSM can perform these cryptographic operations and store these private keys issued by your certificate authority.

Enable transparent data encryption for Oracle databases

Oracle databases offer a feature called transfer data encryption for encrypting data before storing it on disk. This feature is available in some versions of Oracle. It uses a two-tier key structure for securing encryption keys. Data is encrypted using the table key and this table key is encrypted by using the master key. CloudHSM can be used to store this master encryption key.

Amazon Macie

Amazon Macie is the newest security service powered by Artificial Intelligence launched by AWS that uses machine learning to identify, categorize, and secure your sensitive data that is stored in S3 buckets. It continuously monitors your data and sends alerts when it detects an anomaly in the usage or access patterns. It uses templated Lambda functions for either sending alerts, revoking unauthorized access, or resetting password policies upon detecting suspicious behavior.

As of now, Amazon Macie supports S3 and CloudTrail with the support for more services such as EC2, DynamoDB, RDS, Glue is planned in the near future. Let us look at two important features of Amazon Macie.

Data discovery and classification

Amazon Macie allows you to discover and classify sensitive data along with analyzing usage patterns and user behavior. It continuously monitors newly added data to your existing data storage.

It uses artificial intelligence to understand and analyze usage patterns of existing data in the AWS environment. It understands data by using the **Natural Language Processing (NLP)** method.

It will classify sensitive data and prioritize it according to your unique organizational data access patterns. You can use it to create your own alerts and policy definitions for securing your data.

Data security

Amazon Macie allows you to be proactively compliant with security and achieve preventive security. It enables you to discover, classify, and secure multiple data types such as personally identifiable information, protected health information, compliance documents, audit reports, encryption keys, API keys, and so on.

You can audit instantly by verifying compliance with logs that are automated. All the changes to ACL and security policies can be identified easily. You can configure actionable alerts to detect changes in user behavior.

You can also configure notifications when your protected data leaves the secured zone. You can detect events when an unusual amount of sensitive data is shared either internally or externally.

Summary

Data security is one of the major requirements for most of the AWS users. The AWS platform provides multiple options to secure data in their data storage services for data at rest and data in transit. We learned about securing data for most popular storage services such as AWS S3, AWS RDS, and so on.

We learned the fundamentals of data encryption and how AWS KMS provides a fully managed solution for creating encryption keys, managing, controlling, and auditing usage of these encryption keys.

We also learned about AWS CloudHSM, a dedicated hardware appliance to store your encryption keys for corporate or regulatory compliance. We went through various features of CloudHSM and the most popular use cases for this service.

Lastly, we went through Amazon Macie, a newly launched data security service that uses machine learning for protecting your critical data by automatically detecting and classifying it.

The AWS EC2 service provides compute or servers in AWS for purposes such as web servers, database servers, application servers, monitoring servers, and so on. The EC2 is offered as IaaS in AWS. In the next chapter, *Securing Servers in AWS*, we will look at options to protect your infrastructure in an AWS environment from various internal and external threats. There are host of AWS services dedicated to secure your servers; we will dive deep into these services.

5
Securing Servers in AWS

The Amazon **Elastic Compute Cloud (EC2)** web service provides secure, elastic, scalable computing capacity in the form of virtual computing environments known as instances in the AWS cloud. EC2 is the backbone of AWS, in a way, so that it drives a majority of the revenue for AWS. This service enables users to run their web applications on a cloud by renting servers. EC2 is part of the **Infrastructure as a Service (IaaS)** offering from AWS, and it provides complete control over the instance provided to the user.

These servers or instances are used for a variety of use cases, such as running web applications, installing various software, running databases, and file storage. EC2 has various benefits that make it quite popular:

- Secured service offering multiple options for securing servers
- Elastic web scale computing; no need to guess the computing capacity
- Complete control over your EC2 instance
- Multiple instance types for various scenarios
- Integration with other AWS services
- Reliable service, offering 99.95% availability for each region
- Inexpensive, offering pay-what-you-use and pay-as-you-use models

Since most of the workloads in AWS run or use EC2 one way or another, it is critical to secure your servers. AWS provides multiple options to secure your servers from numerous threats and gives you the ability to test these security measures as well. Securing servers is essentially securing your infrastructure in AWS. It involves accessing your EC2 instances, monitoring activities on your EC2 instances, and protecting them from external threats such as hacking, **Distributed Denial of Service (DDoS)** attacks, and so on.

With the Amazon EC2 service, users can launch virtual machines with various configurations in the AWS cloud. AWS users have full control over these elastic and scalable virtual machines, also known as EC2 instances.

In this chapter, you are going to learn about best practices and ways to secure EC2 instances in the cloud. AWS provides security for EC2 instances at multiple levels, such as in the operating system of the physical host, in the operating system of the virtual machine, and through multiple firewalls to ensure all API calls are signed. Each of these security measures is built on the capabilities of other security measures.

Our goal is to secure data stored and transferred from an AWS EC2 instance so that it reaches its destination without being intercepted by malicious systems while also maintaining the flexibility of the AWS EC2 instance, along with other AWS services. Our servers in AWS should always be protected from ever-evolving threats and vulnerabilities.

We will dive deep into the following areas of EC2 security:

- IAM roles for EC2
- Managing OS-level access to Amazon EC2 instances
- Protecting the system from malware
- Securing your infrastructure
- Intrusion detection and prevention systems
- Elastic load balancing security
- Building threat protection layers
- Test security

In Chapter 3, *AWS Virtual Private Cloud*, we looked at ways to secure your network in the AWS cloud. We looked at **network access control list (NACL)** and security groups as two firewalls provided by AWS for subnets and EC2 instances, respectively. In this chapter, we are going to dig deeper into security groups. We will also look at other ways to protect your infrastructure in the cloud.

We will look into AWS Inspector, an agent-based and API-driven service that automatically assesses security and vulnerabilities for applications deployed on EC2 instances. We will cover the following topics for AWS Inspector service:

- Features and benefits
- Components

Next, you will learn about AWS Shield, a managed DDoS protection service that will help you minimize downtime and latency for your applications running on EC2 instances and for your AWS resources, such as EC2 instances, **Elastic Load Balancer** (**ELB**), Route 53, and so on. We will cover the following topics for the AWS Shield service:

- Benefits
- Key features

EC2 Security best practices

There are general best practices for securing EC2 instances that are applicable irrespective of operating system or whether instances are running on virtual machines or on on-premise data centers. Let's look at these general best practices:

- **Least access**: Unless required, ensure that your EC2 instance has restricted access to the instance, as well as restricted access to the network. Provide access only to trusted entities, including software and operating system components that are required to be installed on these instances.
- **Least privilege**: Always follow the principle of least privilege required by your instances, as well as users, to perform their functions. Use role-based access for your instances and create roles with limited permissions. Control and monitor user access for your instances.
- **Configuration management**: Use AWS configuration management services to have a baseline for your instance configuration and treat each EC2 instance as a configuration item. This base configuration should include the updated version of your anti-virus software, security patches, and so on. Keep assessing the configuration of your instance against baseline configuration periodically. Make sure you are generating, storing, and processing logs and audit data.
- **Change management**: Ensure that automated change management processes are in place in order to detect changes in the server configuration. Create rules using AWS services to roll back any changes that are not in line with accepted server configuration or changes that are not authorized.
- **Audit logs**: Ensure that all changes to the server are logged and audited. Use AWS logging and auditing features, such as AWS CloudTrail and VPC flow logs, for logging all API requests and AWS VPC network traffic, respectively.

- **Network access**: AWS provides three options to secure network access for your EC2 instances, security groups, network access control lists, and route tables. An **Elastic Network Interface (ENI)** connected to your instance provides network connectivity to an AWS VPC.

  - Configure security group rules to allow minimum traffic for your instance. For example, if your EC2 instance is a web server, allow only HTTP and HTTPS traffic.

  - Use network access control lists as a second layer of defense, as these are stateless and needs more maintenance. Use them to deny traffic from unwanted sources.

  - Configure route tables for the subnet in your VPC to ensure that instance-specific conditions are met by distinct route tables. For example, create a route table for internet access and associate it with all subnets that require access to the internet.

- **AWS API access from EC2 instances**: Quite often, applications running on EC2 instances would need to access multiple AWS services programmatically by making API calls. AWS recommends that you create roles for these applications, as roles are managed by AWS and credentials are rotated multiple times in a day. Moreover, with roles, there is no need to store credentials locally on an EC2 instance.

- **Data encryption**: Any data that is either stored on or transmitted through an EC2 instance should be encrypted. Use **Elastic Block Storage (EBS)** volumes to encrypt your data at rest through the AWS **Key Management Service (KMS)**. To secure data in transit through encryption, use **Transport Layer Security (TLS)** or IPsec encryption protocols. Ensure that all connections to your EC2 instances are encrypted by configuring outbound rules for security groups.

EC2 Security

An EC2 instance comprises many components: the most prominent ones are the **Amazon Machine Image (AMI)**, the preconfigured software template for your server containing the operating system and software; the hardware including the processor, memory, storage, and networking components based on your requirements; persistent or ephemeral storage volumes for storing your data; the IP addresses, VPCs and virtual and physical location for your instance, such as its subnet, availability zone, and regions, respectively.

When an instance is launched, it is secured by creating a key pair and configuring the security group, a virtual firewall for your instance. In order to access your instance, you will be required to authenticate using this key pair, as depicted in the following figure:

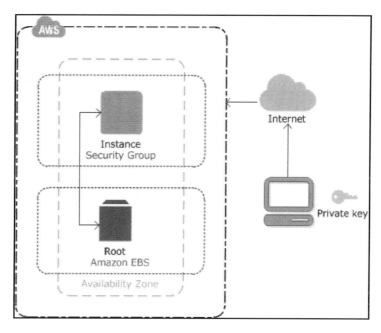

Figure 1 - AWS EC2 security

EC2 instances interact with various AWS services and cater to multiple scenarios and use cases across industries, and this universal usability opens up a host of security vulnerabilities for an EC2 instance. AWS provides options for addressing all such vulnerabilities. Let's look at all of these options in detail.

IAM roles for EC2 instances

If an application is running on an EC2 instance, it must pass credentials along with its API request. These credentials can be stored in the EC2 instance and managed by developers. Developers have to ensure that these credentials are securely passed to every EC2 instance and are rotated for every instance as well. This is a lot of overhead, which leaves room for errors and security breaches at multiple points.

Alternatively, you can use IAM roles for this purpose. IAM roles provide temporary credentials for accessing AWS resources. IAM roles do not store credentials on instances, and credentials are managed by AWS, so they are automatically rotated multiple times in a day. When an EC2 instance is launched, it is assigned an IAM role. This role will have required permissions to access the desired AWS resource. You can also attach an IAM role to an instance while it is running.

In the following figure, an IAM role to access an S3 bucket is created for an EC2 instance. The developer launches an instance with this role. The application running on this instance uses temporary credentials to access content in the S3 bucket.

In this scenario, the developer is not using long-term credentials that are stored in EC2 instances, thus making this transaction more secure:

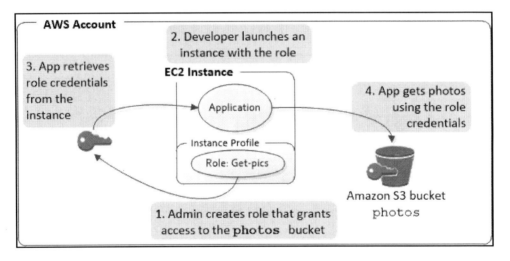

Figure 2 - IAM role for EC2 instance

Managing OS-level access to Amazon EC2 instances

Accessing the operating system of an EC2 instance requires different credentials than applications running on an EC2 instance. AWS lets you use your own credentials for the operating system; however, AWS helps you to bootstrap for initial access to the operating system. You can access the operating system of your instance using secure remote system access protocols such as Windows **Remote Desktop Protocol (RDP)** or **Secure Shell (SSH)**.

You can set up the following methods for authenticating operating system access:

- X.509 certificate authentication
- Local operating system accounts
- Microsoft active directory

AWS provides key pairs for enabling authentication to the EC2 instance. These keys can be generated by AWS or by you; AWS stores the public key, and you store the private key. You can have multiple key pairs for authenticating access to multiple instances. For enhanced security, you can also use LDAP or active directory authentication as alternative methods for authentication, instead of the AWS key pair authentication mechanism.

Protecting your instance from malware

An instance in the AWS cloud should be protected from malware (that is, viruses, trojans, spams, and so on), just like any server would be protected in your data center. Having an instance infected with a malware can have far-reaching implications on your entire infrastructure on the cloud.

When a user runs code on an EC2 instance, this executable code assumes the privileges of this user and it can carry out any action that can be carried out by this user based on the user privileges. So, as a rule of thumb, always run code that is trusted and verified with proper code review procedures on your EC2 instances.

If you are using an AMI to launch an EC2 instance, you must ensure this AMI is safe and trusted. Similarly, always install and run trusted software; download this software from trusted and established entities. You could create software depots for all your trusted software and prevent users from downloading software from random sources on the internet.

Ensure all your public facing instances and applications are patched with the latest security configurations and that these patches are revisited regularly and frequently. An infected instance can be used to send spam, a large number of unsolicited emails. This scenario can be prevented by avoiding SMTP open relay (insecure relay or third-party relay), which is usually used to spread spam.

Always keep your antivirus software, along with your anti-spam software updated from reputed and trusted sources on your EC2 instance.

In the event of your instance getting infected, use your antivirus software to remove the virus. Back up all your data and reinstall all the software, including applications, platforms, and so on, from a trusted source, and restore data from your backup. This approach is recommended and widely used in the event of an infected EC2 instance.

Secure your infrastructure

AWS lets you create your own virtual private network in the AWS cloud, as you learned in Chapter 3, *AWS Virtual Private Cloud*. VPC enables you to secure your infrastructure on the cloud using multiple options, such as security groups, network access control lists, route tables, and so on. Along with securing infrastructure, VPC also allows you to establish a secure connection with your data center outside of the AWS cloud or with your infrastructure in other AWS accounts. These connections could be through AWS direct connect or through the internet.

Security groups should be used to control traffic allowed for an instance or group of instances performing similar functions, such as web servers or database servers. A security group is a virtual, instance-level firewall. It is assigned to an instance when an instance is launched. You could assign more than one security group to an instance. Rules of security groups can be changed anytime, and they are applied immediately to all instances attached to that security group.

AWS recommends that you use security groups as the first line of defense for an EC2 instance. Security groups are stateful, so responses for an allowed inbound rule will always be allowed irrespective of the outbound rule, and if an instance sends a request, the response for that request will be allowed irrespective of inbound rule configuration.

The following figure shows a security group `SL-Web-SG` configured for all web servers inside a VPC. There are three rules configured; HTTP and HTTPS traffic are allowed from the internet, and SSH for accessing this instance is allowed only from a public IP, that is, `118.185.136.34`:

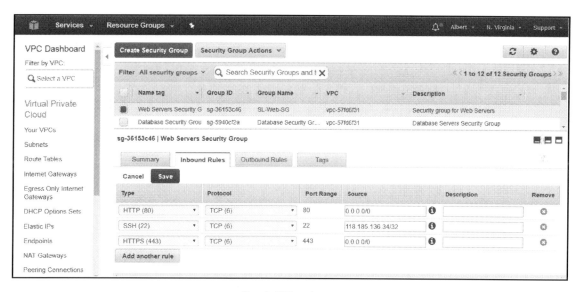

Figure 3 - AWS security groups

Each AWS account has a default security group for the default VPC in every region. If you do not specify a security group for your instance, this default security group automatically gets associated with your EC2 instance. This default security group allows all inbound traffic from instances where the source is this default security group. Alongside, it allows all outbound traffic from your EC2 instance. You can modify rules for this default security group, but you cannot delete it.

Security groups are versatile in nature; they allow multiple options for sources for inbound access and destinations for outbound access. Apart from the IP address or range of IP addresses, you can also enter another security group as an object reference for source or destination in order to allow traffic for instances in your security group. However, this process will not add any rules to the current security group from the source security group.

The following figure depicts this example, where we have a security group for database servers; this security group allows traffic only from a web servers security group. In this configuration, the web servers security group is an object reference for the source field, so all the instances that are associated with the database security group will always allow traffic from all instances associated with the web servers security group:

Figure 4 - AWS security groups object reference

Intrusion Detection and Prevention Systems

An **Intrusion Detection System (IDS)** is a detective and monitoring control that continuously scans your network, servers, platform, and systems for any security breach or violation of security policy, such as a configuration change or malicious activity. If it detects an anomaly, it will report it to the security team.

An **Intrusion Prevention System (IPS)**, on the other hand, is a preventive control. These controls are placed inside your network, behind organizations' firewalls, and act as a firewall for all known issues and threats related to incoming traffic. All traffic needs to pass IPS in order to reach their destination. If an IPS finds traffic to contain malicious content, it will block that traffic.

The AWS marketplace offers various IDS and IPS products to secure your network and systems. These products help you detect vulnerabilities in your EC2 instances by deploying host-based IDS and by employing behavioral monitoring techniques.

These products also help you secure your AWS EC2 instances from attacks by deploying next-generation firewalls in your network, which have features such as full stack visibility for all layers in your infrastructure.

Elastic Load Balancing Security

An **Elastic Load Balancer** (ELB) is a managed AWS service that automatically distributes incoming traffic to targets behind a load balancer across all availability zones in a region. These targets could be EC2 instances, containers, and IP addresses.

An ELB takes care of all encryption and decryption centrally, so there is no additional workload on EC2 instances. An ELB can be associated with AWS VPC and has its own security groups. These security groups can be configured in a similar way to EC2 security groups with inbound and outbound rules.

Alongside, ELB also supports end-to-end traffic encryption through the **Transport Layer Security** (TLS) protocol for networks using HTTPS connections. In this scenario, you don't need to use an individual instance for terminating client connections while using TLS; instead, you can use ELB to perform the same function. You can create an HTTPS listener for your ELB that will encrypt traffic between your load balancer and clients initiating HTTPS sessions. It will also encrypt traffic between EC2 instances and load balancers serving traffic to these EC2 instances.

Building Threat Protection Layers

Quite often, organizations will have multiple features for securing their infrastructure, network, data, and so on. The AWS cloud gives you various such features in the form of VPC, security groups as virtual firewall for your EC2 instances, NACL as secondary firewalls for your subnets, and host-based firewalls and IDS, along with **Intrusion Prevention System** (IPS), for creating your own threat protection layer as part of your security framework.

This threat protection layer will prevent any unwanted traffic from reaching its desired destination, such as an application server or a database server. For example, in the following figure, a corporate user is accessing an application from the corporate data center. This user is connecting to AWS VPC using a secure connection, which could be a VPN connection or a direct connect connection and does not require interception by a threat protection layer.

However, requests made by all users accessing this application through the internet are required to go through a threat protection layer before they reach the presentation layer.

This approach is known as layered network defense on the cloud. This approach is suitable for organizations that need more than what AWS offers out of the box for protecting networking infrastructure. AWS VPC provides you with various features to support the building of your threat protection layer; these features include the following:

- Support for multiple layers of load balancers
- Support for multiple IP addresses
- Support for multiple **Elastic Network Interfaces (ENI)**

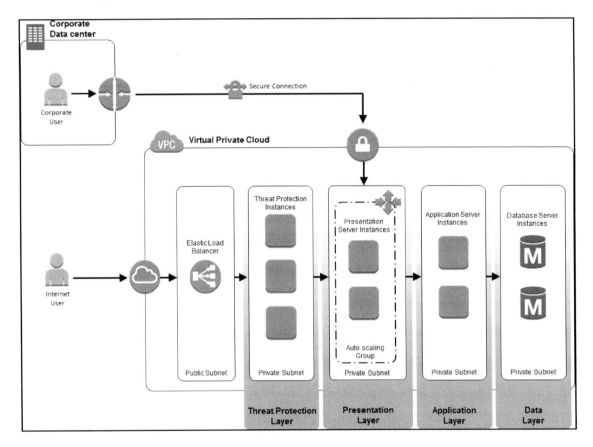

Figure 5 - AWS layered network defense

Testing security

It is imperative for any **Infrastructure Security Management System (ISMS)** to continuously test their security measures and validate them against ever-evolving threats and vulnerabilities. Testing these security measures and controls involves testing the infrastructure and network provided by AWS. AWS recommends that you take the following approaches to test the security of your environment:

- **External vulnerability assessment**: Engage a third party that has no knowledge of your infrastructure and controls deployed. Let this third party test all your controls and systems independently. Use the findings of this engagement to strengthen your security framework.
- **External penetration tests**: Utilize the services of a third party that has no knowledge of your infrastructure and controls deployed to break into your network and servers in a controlled manner. Use these findings to strengthen your security controls deployed for intrusion prevention.
- **Internal gray or white-box review of applications and platforms**: Use an internal resource, a tester, who has knowledge of your security controls to try to break into the security of applications and platforms and expose or discover vulnerabilities.
- **Penetration testing process**: AWS allows you to conduct penetration testing for your own instances; however, you have to request permission from AWS before you conduct any penetration testing. You would have to log in using root credentials for the instance that you want to test and fill an AWS Vulnerability/Penetration Testing Request Form. If you want a third party to conduct these tests, you can fill the details about it in this form as well.

As of now, the AWS penetration testing policy allows testing of the following AWS services:

- Amazon Elastic Compute Cloud
- Amazon Relational Database Service
- Amazon Aurora
- Amazon CloudFront
- Amazon API Gateway
- AWS Lambda
- AWS Lightsail
- DNS Zone Walking

Amazon Inspector

Amazon Inspector is an automated, agent-based security and vulnerability assessment service for your AWS resources. As of now, it supports only EC2 instances. It essentially complements devops culture in an organization, and it integrates with continuous integration and continuous deployment tools.

To begin with, you install an agent in your EC2 instance, prepare an assessment template, and run a security assessment for this EC2 instance.

Amazon Inspector will collect data related to running processes, the network, the filesystem and lot of data related to configuration, the traffic flow between AWS services and network, the secure channels, and so on.

Once this data is collected, it is validated against a set of predefined rules known as the rules package, that you choose in your assessment template, and you are provided with detailed findings and issues related to security, categorized by severity.

The following figure shows the Amazon Inspector splash screen with three steps for getting started with Amazon Inspector:

Figure 6 - Amazon Inspector splash screen

Amazon Inspector features and benefits

Amazon Inspector goes hand in hand with the continuous integration and continuous deployment activities that are essential part of the DevOps life cycle. It helps you integrate security with your DevOps by making security assessment part of your deployment cycle. Amazon Inspector has several important features that make it one of the most preferred security assessment services for any infrastructure in AWS. Let's look at these features:

- **Enforce security standards and compliance**: You can select a security best practices rules package to enforce the most common security standards for your infrastructure. Ensure that assessments are run before any deployment to proactively detect and address security issues before they reach the production environment. You can ensure that security compliance standards are met at every stage of your development life cycle. Moreover, Amazon Inspector provides findings based on real activity and the actual configuration of your AWS resources, so you can rest assured about the compliance of your environment.

- **Increasing development agility**: Amazon Inspector is fully automatable through API. Once you integrate it with your development and deployment process, your security issues and your vulnerabilities are detected and resolved early, resulting in saving a huge amount of resources. These resources can be used to develop new features for your application and release it to your end users, thus increasing the velocity of your development.

- **Leverage AWS Security expertise**: Amazon Inspector is a managed service, so when you select a rules package for assessment, you get assessed for the most updated security issues and vulnerabilities for your EC2 instance. Moreover, these rules packages are constantly updated with ever evolving threats, vulnerabilities, and best practices by the AWS Security organization.

- **Integrated with AWS services and AWS partners**: Amazon Inspector integrates with AWS partners, providing security tools through its public-facing APIs. AWS partners use Amazon Inspector's findings to create email alerts, security status dashboards, pager platforms, and so on. Amazon Inspector works with a **network address translation** (**NAT**) instance, as well as proxy environments. It also integrates with the AWS **Simple Notification Service** (**SMS**) for notifications and AWS CloudTrail for recording all API activity.

The following figure shows the Amazon Inspector integration with AWS CloudTrail. All activities related to Amazon Inspector are captured by AWS CloudTrail events:

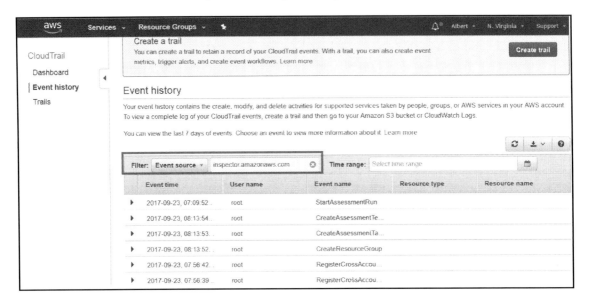

Figure 7 - Amazon Inspector CloudTrail events

Amazon Inspector publishes real-time metrics data to AWS CloudWatch so you can analyze metrics for your target (EC2 instance) as well as for your assessment template in AWS CloudWatch. By default, Amazon Inspector sends data to AWS CloudWatch in interval of five minutes. It could be changed to a one minute interval as well.

There are three categories of metrics available in AWS CloudWatch for Amazon Inspector, as follows:

- Assessment target
- Assessment template
- Aggregate

The following figure shows metrics available for assessment targets in AWS CloudWatch:

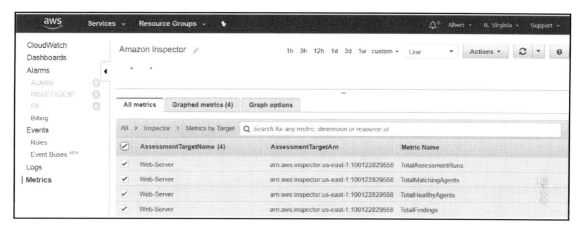

Figure 8 - Amazon Inspector CloudWatch metrics

Amazon Inspector components

Amazon Inspector is accessible the through AWS Management Console, the AWS **Software Development Kit (SDK)**, AWS Command Line Tools, and Amazon Inspector APIs, through HTTPS. Let's look at the major components of this service, as shown in the following figure:

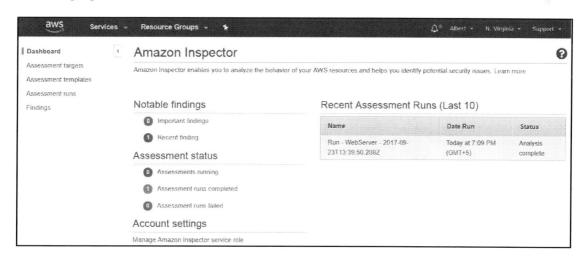

Figure 9 - Amazon Inspector dashboard

- **AWS agent**: This is a software agent developed by AWS that must be installed in your assessment target, that is, your EC2 instance. This agent monitors all activities and collects data for your EC2 instance, such as the installation, configuration, and filesystem, as per the rules package selected by you for assessment. It periodically sends this data to the Amazon Inspector service. AWS Agent simply collects data; it does not change anything in the EC2 instance it is running.
- **Assessment run**: You will periodically run assessments on your EC2 instance based on the rules package selected. Once your AWS agent performs assessment, it discovers any security vulnerabilities in your EC2 instance. Once you have completed the assessment, you will get findings, with a list of potential issues and their severity.
- **Assessment target**: Amazon Inspect or requires you to select an assessment target; this is your EC2 instance or a group of EC2 instances that will be assessed for any potential security issues. These instances should be tagged with key value pairs. You can create up to 50 assessment targets per AWS account.
- **Finding**: A finding is a potential security issue reported by Amazon Inspector service after running an assessment for your target EC2 instance. These findings are displayed in the Amazon Inspector web console or can be accessed through API. These findings contain details about the issue, along with its severity and recommendations to fix it.
- **Assessment report**: This is a document that details what all was tested for an assessment, along with the results of those tests. You can generate assessment reports for all assessments once they are completed successfully. There are two types of assessment reports:
    - The findings report
    - The full report
- **Rules package**: Amazon Inspector has a repository of hundreds of rules, divided under four rules packages. These rules packages are the knowledge base of the most common security and vulnerability definitions. Your assessment target is checked against the rules of a rules package. These rules packages are constantly updated by the Amazon security team, as and when new threats, security issues, and vulnerabilities are identified or discovered. These four rules packages are shown in the following figure:

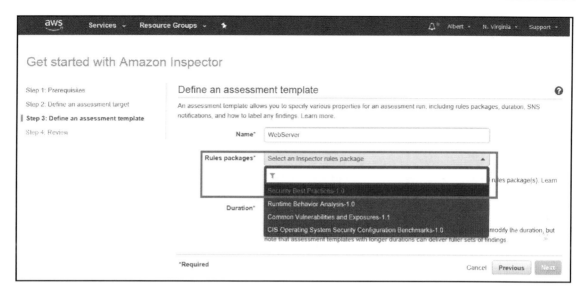

Figure 10 - Amazon Inspector rules packages

- **Rules**: Amazon Inspector has predefined rules in the rules packages; as of now, custom rules cannot be defined for a rules package. A rule is a check performed by an Amazon Inspector agent on an assessment target during an assessment. If a rule finds a security issue, it will add this issue to findings. Every rule has a security level assigned to it. There are four security levels for a rule, as follows:
  - High
  - Medium
  - Low
  - Informational

  A high, medium, or low security level indicates an issue that might cause an interruption in the ways in which your services are required to run. An informational security level describes the security configuration for your instance.

- **Assessment template**: This is your configuration for running an assessment. You will choose your targets, along with one of the four predefined rules packages that you want to run; you will also choose a duration, from 15 minutes to 24 hours, and other information, as shown in the following figure:

Figure 11 - Amazon Inspector assessment template

AWS Shield

AWS Shield is a managed **Distributed Denial of Service (DDoS)** protection service. It detects and automatically mitigates attacks that could potentially result in downtime for your application and might also increase latency for your applications running on EC2 instances.

A DDoS attack results in increased traffic for your EC2 instances, Elastic Load Balancer, Route 53, or CloudFront. As a result, these services would need to scale up resources to cope with the increased traffic. A DDoS attack usually happens when multiple systems are compromised or infected with a Trojan flooding a target system with an intention to deny a service to intended users by generating traffic and shutting down a resource so it cannot serve more requests.

AWS Shield has two tiers: **Standard** and **Advanced**. All protection under the AWS Shield Standard option is available to all AWS customers by default, without any additional charge. The AWS Shield Advanced option is available to customers with business and enterprise support at an additional charge. The advanced option provides protection against more sophisticated attacks on your AWS resources, such as an EC2 instance, ELB, and so on. The following figure shows AWS Shield tiers:

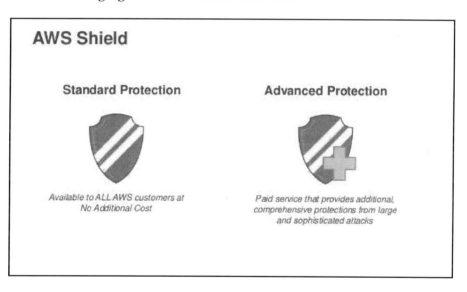

Figure 12 - AWS shield tiers

AWS Shield benefits

AWS Shield is covered under the AWS suite of services that are eligible for **Health Insurance Portability and Accounting Act (HIPAA)** compliance. It can be used to protect websites hosted outside of AWS, as it is integrated with AWS CloudFront. Let's look at other benefits of AWS Shield:

- **Seamless integration and deployment**: AWS Shield Standard automatically secures your AWS resources with the most common and regular DDoS attacks in network and transport layers. If you require enhanced security for more sophisticated attacks, you can opt for the AWS Shield Advanced option for your AWS resources, such as EC2 Instances, Route 53 AWS CloudFront, and so on, by enabling the AWS Shield Advanced option from the AWS Management Console or through APIs.

- **Customizable protection**: You can script your own customized rules to address sophisticated attacks on your AWS resources using the AWS Shield Advanced tier. You can deploy these rules immediately to avoid any imminent threat, such as by blocking bad traffic or for automating response to security incidents. You could also take the help of the AWS **DDoS Response Team (DRT)** to write the rules for you. This team is available for your support 24/7.

- **Cost efficient**: AWS provides free protection against network layer attacks for all its customers through AWS Shield Standard. With AWS Shield Advanced, you get protection against DDoS Cost Escalation, which prevents your cost going up in case of DDoS attacks. However, if you are billed for any of your AWS resource usage due to a DDoS attack, you can request credits from AWS through the AWS support channel.

The AWS Shield Advanced billing plan starts at USD $3000 per month. Charges for data transfer are calculated separately for all AWS resources selected for the AWS Shield advanced protection.

AWS Shield features

Let's look at AWS Shield features for Standard and Advanced tiers.

AWS Shield Standard

- **Quick detection**: AWS Shield Standard automatically inspects all traffic for your AWS resources through its continuous network flow monitoring feature. It detects any malicious traffic through a combination of advanced algorithms, specific analysis, traffic signatures, and so on in real time, to prevent you from the most common and frequent attacks.
- **Inline attack mitigation**: AWS Shield Standard gives you protection against Layer 3 and Layer 4 attacks that occur at the infrastructure layer through its automated mitigation processes. These processes do not have any impact on performance, such as the latency of your AWS resources, as they are applied inline for your applications. Inline mitigation helps you avoid the downtime for your AWS resources and your applications running on these AWS resources.

AWS Shield Advanced

Enhanced detection: This feature helps with detecting DDoS attacks on the application layer, such as HTTP floods, as well as with monitoring and verifying network traffic flow.

Advanced attack mitigation: For protection against large DDoS attacks, AWS Shield advanced provides protection automatically by applying advanced routing processes. You also have access to the AWS **DDoS Response Team (DRT)**, which can help you mitigate more sophisticated and advanced DDoS attacks manually. DRT can work with you to diagnose and manually mitigate attacks on your behalf.

You can also enable AWS Shield advanced on your multiple AWS accounts as long as all of these accounts are under one single billing account and are owned by you, and all AWS resources in these accounts are owned by you.

With AWS Shield advanced, you get a history of all incidents in your AWS account for the past 13 months. As it is integrated with AWS CloudWatch, you get a notification through AWS CloudWatch metrics as soon as an attack happens. This notification will be sent in a matter of a few minutes.

Summary

In this chapter, you learned about various features and services available in AWS to secure your servers, most notably, EC2 instances. We went through best practices to follow for EC2 security.

Alongside, we dove deep into various measures to follow for all use cases for securing your EC2 instances. These measures range from using IAM roles for all applications running on EC2 instances to managing operating system access to building threat protection layers in your multi-layered architectures and testing security for your EC2 instances with prior permission from AWS support.

You learned about Amazon Inspector, an automated security assessment managed service that integrates security assessment, identification, and remediation with development. This results in faster deployment and better agility for your development process. You learned about the various components of Amazon Inspector, such as agents, assessment template, findings, and so on, to help use this service for EC2 instances.

Lastly, we went through AWS Shield, a managed DDoS protection service, along with its features and benefits. You learned about the AWS Shield tiers, Standard and Advanced, and how they can protect AWS resources from the most common, as well as the most advanced and sophisticated, attacks. In this section, you learned about AWS DRT, a team available 24/7 to help us mitigate attacks and respond to incidents that can also write code for us if required.

In the next chapter, *Securing Applications in AWS*, you are going to learn about various AWS services provided to AWS customers for securing applications running on AWS. These could be a monolithic application, a web or a mobile application, a serverless application, or a microservices-based application. These applications could run entirely on AWS, or they could run in a hybrid mode, that is, partially in AWS and partially outside of AWS.

These applications might run on various AWS resources and interact with various AWS resources, such as applications running on EC2 instances that store data on AWS S3. This scenario opens up the possibility of attacks from various channels. AWS has a whole suite of services and features to thwart all such attacks, including application-level firewalls, managed services for user authentication, managed services for securing APIs, and so on.

6
Securing Applications in AWS

AWS gives you multiple services, features, and tools to build scalable, de-coupled, and secure cloud applications. AWS supports web application development in programming languages such as Python, JAVA, .NET, PHP, Ruby, and mobile application development as well as Android and iOS platforms by providing **Software Development Kits (SDKs)**. Alongside this, it provides the following tools for developing applications in the AWS cloud environment:

- **Integrated development environments (IDEs)** such as Visual Studio and Eclipse
- Command-line tools such as AWS CLI, AWS tools for PowerShell, and so on
- Services for running these applications, such as Elastic Compute Cloud, AWS Elastic Beanstalk, and Amazon EC2 Container Service
- Tools and services for developing serverless applications such as AWS **Serverless Application Model (SAM)** and AWS Lambda respectively
- Managed services such as AWS CodeCommit for source control and AWS CodeDeploy for automation of code deployment process

When you develop and deploy web and mobile applications in the cloud using the above-mentioned services, tools, and features, you need to secure it from SQL injections, unwanted traffic, intrusions, **Distributed Denial of Service (DDoS)** attacks, and other similar threats. Furthermore, you need to ensure that all requests sent to AWS through your applications are secure and recognized by AWS as authorized requests. Your applications that are deployed on EC2 instances should be able to communicate securely with other AWS services such as the **Simple Storage Service (S3)** or **Relational Database Service (RDS)**. Securing applications in AWS is as critical as securing your data and infrastructure in AWS.

In this chapter, we will learn about securing web and mobile applications in AWS cloud. We will begin with **Web Application Firewall (WAF)**, an AWS service that secures your web applications from common threats by creating access control lists to filter threats. We will learn the following about AWS WAF:

- Benefits of AWS WAF
- Working with AWS WAF
- Security automation with AWS WAF

Moving on we will walk you through securing API requests by learning to sign these requests while communicating with AWS services and resources.

Furthermore, we will learn about a couple of AWS services, as follows, that are extremely useful in securing our applications in the cloud.

- **Amazon Cognito**: A managed AWS service for authenticating user data for your mobile applications.
- **Amazon API Gateway**: A managed AWS service for securing, creating, and managing APIs.

AWS Web Application Firewall (WAF)

AWS WAF is a web application firewall that helps you define various rules in the form of conditions and access control lists to secure your web applications from common security threats, such as cross-site scripting, DDoS attacks, SQL injections, and so on. These threats may result in application unavailability or an application consuming excessive resources due to an increase in malicious web traffic.

You secure your websites and web applications by monitoring, controlling, and filtering HTTP and HTTPS requests received by the Application Load Balancer and Amazon CloudFront. You can allow or reject these requests based on various filters, such as the IP address sending these requests, header values, URI strings, and so on. These security features do not impact the performance of your web applications.

AWS WAF enables you to perform three behaviors--allowing all requests other than the ones that are specified by the access control lists; blocking all requests other than the ones that have been allowed access by the access control lists; counting all requests that are allowable as per the rules set in access control lists. You can use AWS WAF to secure websites hosted outside of the AWS cloud environment, as Amazon CloudFront supports origins outside of AWS. You can configure the Amazon CloudFront to display a custom error page when a request matches your WAF rule and then block it.

It is integrated with CloudWatch and CloudTrail so you can monitor the WAF metrics in real time, such as the number of blocked requests and near real-time and historical audit logs of WAF API respectively. The following figure shows the AWS WAF workflow:

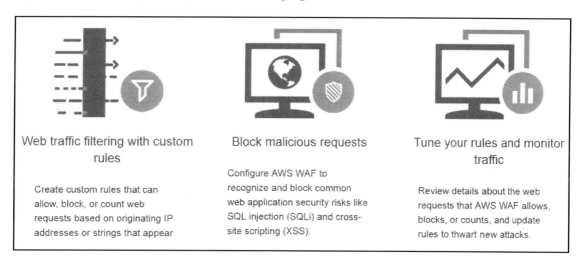

Figure 1 - AWS Web Application Firewall

Benefits of AWS WAF

Let us look at the most popular benefits of AWS WAF:

- **Increased protection against web attacks**: You get protection for your web applications through AWS WAF. It will filter the web traffic based on the access control lists and rules that you can configure for most common web exploits, such as blocking specific IP addresses or blocking matching query strings containing malicious web traffic, and so on.
- **Security integrated with how you develop applications**: AWS WAF enables you to configure all of its features through its APIs and through the AWS Management Console. It also imbibes the culture of DevSecOps in your organization as the development team takes ownership of securing applications by using WAF and adding rules at multiple areas and levels throughout the application development cycle. So you have a developer writing code and adding WAF rules, a DevOps engineer that will deploy this code, and a security auditor who will audit all application security in place of web applications.

- **Ease of deployment and maintenance**: AWS WAF is integrated with Amazon CloudFront and the Application Load Balancer. This makes it easy for you to deploy web applications by making them part of your **Content Delivery Network (CDN)** or by using the Application Load Balancer that is used to front all your web servers. You do not need to install any additional software on any servers or anywhere in your AWS environment. Moreover, you can write rules in one place and deploy them across all your web applications hosted across various resources in your AWS environment.

- **Improved web traffic visibility**: You can set up metrics and dashboards for all your web application requests that are evaluated against your WAF rules in Amazon CloudWatch. You can monitor these metrics in near real-time and gauge the health of your web traffic. You can also use this metrics information to modify the existing WAF rules or create new ones.

- **Cost effective web application development**: AWS WAF prevents you from creating, managing, and deploying your own custom web monitoring and firewall solution. It allows you to save development costs for your custom web application firewall solution. AWS WAF, like other AWS services, allows you to pay only for what you use without any upfront commitment or a minimum fee. It has a flexible pricing model depending on the number of rules deployed and traffic received by your web application in terms of HTTP and HTTPS requests.

Working with AWS WAF

When working with AWS WAF, you begin by creating conditions for matching malicious traffic; next, you combine one or more of these conditions as rules and these rules are combined as web access control lists. These web access control lists can be associated with one or multiple resources in your AWS environment such as Application Load Balancers or CloudFront web distributions.

Conditions: You can define one of the following conditions available in AWS WAF when you would either want to allow or block requests based on these conditions:

- Cross-site scripting
- Geo match
- IP addresses
- Size constraints
- SQL injection
- String and regex matching

The following figure shows an example of an IP address condition where multiple suspicious IP addresses are listed. You can list one IP address as well as range of IP addresses in your conditions:

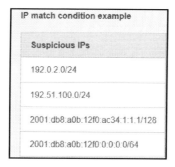

Figure 2 - AWS WAF condition

Rules: You combine conditions to create rules for requests that you want to either allow, block, or count. There are two types of rules:

- **Regular rules**: These rules are created by combining conditions only. For example, a regular rule will contain requests originating from a specific IP address.
- **Rate-based rules**: These rules are similar to regular rules with the addition of a rate limit. Essentially, these rules count the requests every 5 minutes originating from a source and, this enables you to take an action based on the pre-defined rate limit for a rule.

The following diagram shows a couple of rules in the AWS WAF dashboard:

Figure 3 - AWS WAF rules

Web ACL: A set of rules combined together forms a web ACL. You define an action such as allow, block, or count for each rule. Along with these actions, you also define a default action for each rule of your web ACL in scenarios when a request does not meet any of the three conditions for a rule.

The following figure (available in AWS documentation) shows a web ACL containing a rate based rule and regular rules. It also shows how it evaluates the condition for these rules and how it performs actions based on these checks:

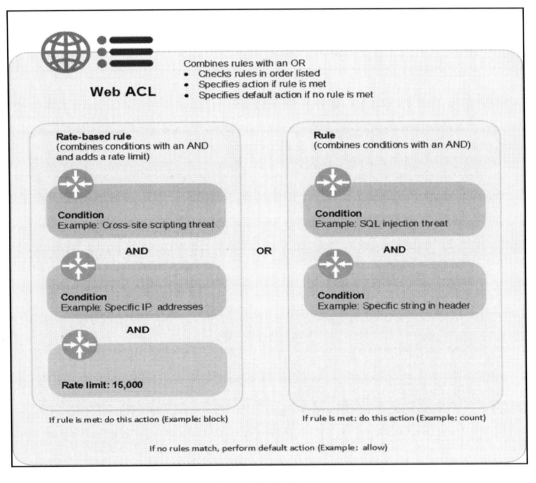

Figure 4 - AWS WAF Web ACL

Signing AWS API requests

API requests sent to AWS should include a digital signature that contains information about the requestor's identity. This identity is verified by AWS for all API requests. This process is known as signing API requests. For all API requests generated through AWS tools, such as AWS SDKs and AWS Command Line Interface, the digital signature is included for you, however, for all API requests that you create manually, you have to include this digital signature yourself.

In other words, you need to sign your HTTP requests when you create them. You need to do this if you are writing a code in a programming language that does not have an AWS SDK. Furthermore, if you need to control what is sent along with an API request, you can choose to sign requests yourself.

A digital signature includes your AWS access keys, that is, your secret access key and access key ID, along with API information. An API request should reach the AWS within 15 minutes of the timestamp stored in this request, otherwise it is rejected by AWS.

There are certain anonymous API requests that do not include digital signatures with identity information, such as anonymous requests to S3 or to API operations requests in the **Security Token Service (STS)**.

Requests are signed to secure your communication with AWS in the following ways:

- Verifying the requestor's identity
- Protecting the data in transit
- Protection against potential replay attacks

AWS recommends using signature version 4 that uses the `HMAC-SHA256` protocol for signing all your requests. It supports signature version 4 and signature version 2.

You sign a request by calculating a hash (digest) for the request. Then you calculate another hash, also known as a signature, by using the previous hash value, information from the request, and your access key. This signature is then added to the request by using either the HTTP Header (authorization) or by adding a query string value to this request.

Amazon Cognito

Amazon Cognito is a managed service that allows you to quickly add users for your mobile and web applications by providing in-built sign-in screens and authentication functionality. It handles security, authorization, and synchronization for your user management process across devices for all your users. You can use Cognito for authenticating your users through external identity providers including social identity providers, such as Facebook, Google, Twitter, LinkedIn, and so on. Cognito can also be used to authenticate identities for any solution that is compatible with SAML 2.0 standard. You can provide temporary security credentials with limited privileges to these authenticated users to securely access your AWS resources. The following figure illustrates three basic functionalities of Amazon Cognito: user management, authentication, and synchronization:

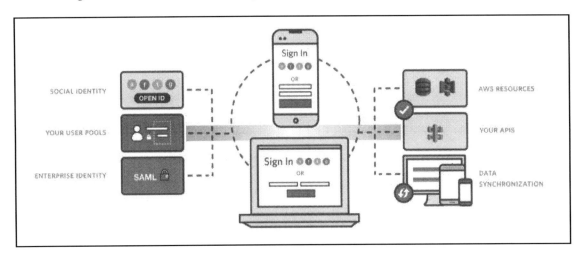

Figure 5 - AWS Cognito overview

This service is primarily designed for developers to use in their web and mobile apps. It enables developers to allow users to securely access the app's resources. You begin by creating and configuring a user pool, a user directory for your apps, in Amazon Cognito either through AWS Management Console, AWS CLI, or through AWS SDK. Once you have created user pool, you can download, install, and integrate AWS Mobile SDK with your app, whether on iOS or Android. You also have an option to call APIs directly for Cognito if you do not wish to use SDK, as it exposes all control and data APIs as web services for you to consume them through your own client library.

Amazon Cognito integrates with CloudTrail and CloudWatch so you can monitor Cognito metrics and log API activities in real time and take the required action for any suspicious activity or security threat.

Amazon API Gateway

As a developer, you have to work with APIs on a regular basis. Amazon API Gateway is a fully managed web service that helps to manage, publish, maintain, monitor, and secure APIs for any workload running on EC2 instances, AWS Lambda, or any web application. You can use API Gateway to manage, authenticate, and secure hundreds of thousands of concurrent API calls. Management of APIs includes access control, traffic management, monitoring, and API version management. All the APIs that are built using API Gateway support data over HTTP protocols. You can also run multiple versions of the same REST API by cloning the existing API. Let us look at the following benefits of using Amazon API Gateway:

- **Low cost and efficient**: You pay for the requests that are made to your API, for example, $3.5 per million API calls, along with the cost of data transfer out, in gigabytes. You also have the option to choose cache for your API, and that will incur charges on an hourly basis. Apart from these, there are no upfront commitments or minimum fees. It integrates with Amazon CloudFront, allowing you access to a global network of Edge locations to run your APIs, resulting in a lower latency of API requests and responses for your end users.

- **Flexible security controls**: With API Gateway, you can use AWS Security and administration services, such as IAM and Cognito, for authorizing access to your APIs. Alternatively, you can also use a custom authorizer, such as Lambda functions, for authentication if you already have OAuth tokens or if you are using other authorization processes. It can also verify signed APIs using the same technology that is used by AWS to verify its own calls.

- **Run your APIs without servers**: API Gateway allows you to run your APIs completely without using any servers through its integration with AWS Lambda. You can run your code entirely in AWS Lambda and use API Gateway to create REST APIs for your web and mobile applications. This allows you to focus on writing code instead of managing to compute resources for your application.

- **Monitor APIs**: You can monitor all your APIs after they have been published and are in use through the API Gateway dashboard. It integrates with Amazon CloudWatch to give you near real-time visibility on the performance of your APIs through metrics, such as data latency, error rates, API calls, and so on. Once you enable detailed monitoring for API Gateway, you can use CloudWatch Logs to receive logs for every API method as well. You can also monitor API utilization by third-party developers through the API Gateway dashboard.

Summary

In this chapter, we learnt about securing applications that are built on top of AWS resources. We went through WAF in detail to protect web applications in AWS and learnt about the benefits and lifecycle of Web Application Firewall. We also walked through the process of automating security with WAF.

Furthermore, we went through the process of signing AWS API requests for securing data in transit along with securing information stored in API itself.

Lastly, we learned about two AWS services that are used by developers to secure their web and mobile applications--Amazon Cognito for user management and Amazon API Gateway for managing and securing APIs.

In next chapter, *Monitoring in AWS*, we will learn about monitoring all AWS resources. Monitoring enables us to gauge operational health, performance, security, and the status of all resources. AWS provides comprehensive monitoring solutions for all web services, resources, and your custom applications to take proactive, preventive and reactive measures in the event of an incident.

7
Monitoring in AWS

Monitoring is an integral part of the information technology environment in all organizations. Monitoring refers to collecting, tracking, and analyzing metrics related to the health and performance of resources, such as infrastructure components and applications, to ensure all resources in an environment are providing services at an acceptable level, that is, that a threshold is set up by resource owners or system administrators. Monitoring these resources allows you to take proactive action in the event of the failure or degradation of a service due to any reason such as a security breach or a DDoS attack. Monitoring is a preventive security measure.

A monitoring service needs to have metrics to monitor, graphs to visualize these metrics and trends, alarms for metrics when thresholds are breached, features to notify and take actions when the state is alarm and most importantly, this service should be able to automate all of the above mentioned features.

AWS has dedicated managed services, features, and solutions in place to meet all your automated and manual monitoring requirements for your simple, standard, distributed, decoupled, and most complex workloads in AWS cloud. Unlike traditional monitoring solutions, AWS offers monitoring solutions while keeping the dynamic nature of cloud implementations in mind. Moreover, most of this monitoring is provided in your basic plan; that means you do not have to pay additional charges to avail these monitoring services.

AWS allows you to monitor all your resources in the cloud such as your servers and your AWS services, along with applications running on these services through its fully managed monitoring service AWS CloudWatch. This service enables you to monitor AWS infrastructure services: container services, platform services, and even abstraction services such as AWS Lambda.

In this chapter, we will learn about the automated and manual monitoring of resources, services, and applications running, and consuming these services in AWS. While these AWS services and AWS resources use similar concepts to traditional resources and services, they work entirely differently. These are elastic in nature; they have the ability to self heal, they are very easy to provision and are mostly configurable, so, monitoring them is a paradigm change for all of us! To monitor the cloud, we need to know how the cloud works! And we are going to learn about monitoring the cloud in this chapter.

We will begin with AWS CloudWatch, a fully managed monitoring service that helps you to monitor all your resources, services, and applications in AWS.

We will learn about features and benefits along with the following components of AWS CloudWatch. While going through these components, we will learn about ways to create these components in detail as well:

- Metrics
- Dashboards
- Events
- Alarms
- Log monitoring

Furthermore, we will walk-through AWS CloudWatch log monitoring and log management capabilities.

Next we will learn about monitoring your servers in AWS, provisioned through AWS EC2 services. Alongside this, we will take a look at monitoring metrics unique to the AWS cloud, such as billing, the **Simple Storage Service** (**S3**), auto scaling, and so on. While going through this section, we are going to see an example of automating your security response by integrating a few AWS services including AWS CloudWatch.

While going through this topic, we will learn about various tools that are available in AWS cloud for automatic and manual monitoring of your EC2 instances. We will deep dive in to the AWS Management Pack for monitoring your applications running on EC2 instances.

Lastly, we will look at the best practices for monitoring your EC2 instances.

AWS CloudWatch

AWS CloudWatch is a monitoring service that collects metrics and tracks them for your resources in AWS, including your applications, in real time. Alongside, you can also collect and monitor log files with AWS CloudWatch. You can set alarms for metrics in AWS CloudWatch to continuously monitor performance, utilization, health, and other parameters of all your AWS resources and take proactive action in the event of metrics crossing thresholds set by resource owners and system administrators. This is accessible through the AWS Management Console, command-line interface, API, and SDKs.

AWS CloudWatch is a global AWS service meaning it can monitor AWS resources and services across all AWS regions. For example, you can monitor EC2 instances available in multiple AWS regions through a single dashboard.

AWS CloudWatch monitors your resources and your applications without installing any additional software. It provides basic monitoring for free that provides data at 5 minute intervals. For an additional charge, you can opt for detailed monitoring that provides data at 1 minute intervals.

AWS CloudWatch has a feature that allows you to publish and retain custom metrics for a 1 second duration for your application, services, and AWS resources. This feature is known as high-resolution custom metrics. You can have your custom metrics publish data either at 1 minute intervals or at 1 second intervals.

The AWS CloudWatch service stores metrics data for a period of 15 months, so even when you have terminated an EC2 instance or deleted an ELB, and you want to look at historical metrics for these resources, you can retrieve them through AWS CloudWatch. You cannot delete stored metrics, they are deleted when they expire after their retention period.

You can watch metrics and statistics through various graphs and dashboards available on the AWS CloudWatch service in the AWS Management Console. These dashboards can be shared to anyone with appropriate permissions. You can view data from multiple regions in one or more dashboards.

The next diagram shows the architecture for AWS CloudWatch. Moving from left to right, we can see that we can work with AWS resources that are integrated with AWS CloudWatch along with custom resources. Metrics for these resources are monitored continuously and stored for a period of 15 months.

These matrices are available to be consumed by AWS services and custom statistics solutions for further analysis. When a metric crosses a threshold, it enters into a state of alarm. This alarm can trigger a notification through the AWS Simple Notification Service to take the required action in response to that alarm. Alternatively, these alarms can also trigger auto scaling actions for your EC2 instances:

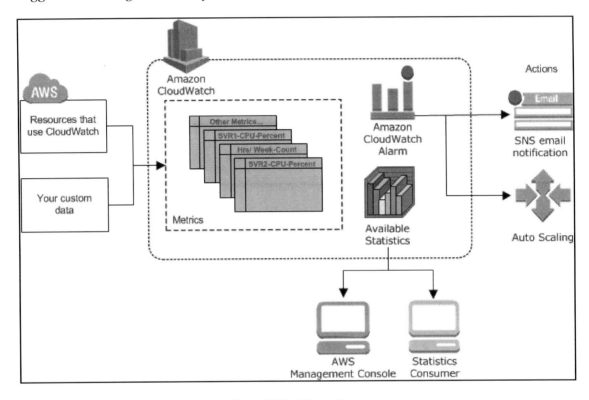

Figure 1 - AWS CloudWatch architecture

Features and benefits

Let us look at most popular features and benefits of AWS CloudWatch:

Monitor EC2: You can monitor the performance and health of all your EC2 instances through native AWS CloudWatch metrics without installing any additional software. These metrics include CPU utilization, network, storage, and so on. You can also create custom metrics such as memory utilization and monitor them with the AWS CloudWatch dashboards.

Monitor other AWS resources: You can monitor other AWS services such as S3, the **Relational Database Service (RDS)**, and DynamoDB, along with AWS billing for billing as per the AWS service and AWS estimated bill for a month without any additional charge. You can also monitor ELB and auto scaling for groups along with EBS volumes for your servers.

Monitor and store logs: You can use AWS CloudWatch to store and process log files for your AWS resources, services, or your applications in near real time. You can also send custom log files to AWS CloudWatch for analysis and troubleshooting. You can search for specific phrases, patterns for behavioral analysis, or values for performance in your log files.

Set alarms: You can set alarms for all your metrics being monitored whenever they cross a threshold. For example, you might want to set an alarm when the CPU utilization for your EC2 instance is above 90% for more than 15 minutes. Moreover, you can also set an alarm for your estimated billing charges as shown in the next screenshot. We have set an alarm for a billing metric called **estimated charges**. The threshold for this metric is set to be greater than US$ 100.

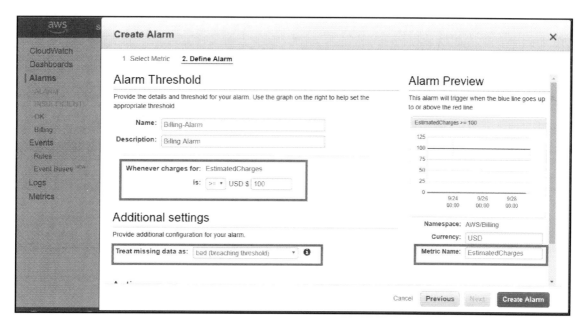

Figure 2 - AWS CloudWatch Create Alarm

Dashboards: You can create dashboards with graphs and statistics for all your resources across multiple AWS regions in one location. These dashboards allow you to set multiple graphs such as line graph, stacked graphs, numbers, or even free flowing text. The following figure shows a dashboard with five sample widgets:

1. CPU utilization for an EC2 instance.
2. Read and write operations per second for EBS volume.
3. Latency and request count metrics for ELB.
4. Object count metrics in an S3 bucket.
5. Estimated charges for the AWS account.

 Note that a metric can be viewed beginning from 1 minute, a few hours, a few days, and a few weeks, and all the way to 15 months. This dashboard can contain information related to resources from all AWS regions. It can be shared with other users as well.

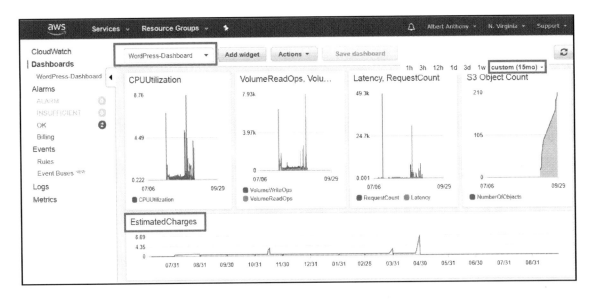

Figure 3 - AWS CloudWatch dashboard

Automate reaction to resource changes: You could use the **Events** option available in AWS CloudWatch to detect events for your AWS resources and respond to these events. These events consist of near real-time information about changes occurring to your AWS resources. You could automate reactions to these events that can self-trigger using cron or rate expressions. These events can be scheduled. You can also integrate AWS events with AWS Lambda functions or AWS **Simple Notification Service** (**SNS**) topics for creating a fully automatic solution.

You can write rules for an event for your application or your AWS services and decide what actions to perform when an event matches your rule.

AWS CloudWatch components

Let us look at the most important components for AWS CloudWatch in detail, including how they work together and how they integrate with other AWS services to create a solution that can automatically respond in the event of a security breach.

Metrics

Metrics is data that you periodically collect for evaluating the health of your resource. A fundamental concept in AWS CloudWatch, a metric is a variable that is monitored, and data points for this metric are its values over a period of time. AWS services send metrics data to AWS CloudWatch and you can send custom metrics for your resources and applications.

Metrics are regional, so they are available only in the region in which they are created. They cannot be deleted; instead they expire after 15 months on a rolling basis if there is no new data published for these metrics. Each metric has a data point, a timestamp, and a unit of measure.

A metric with data point with period of less than 60 seconds is available for 3 hours. Data points with period of 60 seconds are available for 15 days. Data points with period of 300 seconds are available for 63 days and data points with period of 3600 seconds (1 hour) are available for 455 days (15 months).

The collection of metrics data over a period of time is known as statistics. AWS CloudWatch gives statistics based on metrics data provided either by AWS services or custom data provided by you. Following statistics are available in AWS CloudWatch:

- Minimum
- Maximum
- Sum
- Average
- SampleCount
- pNN.NN (value of percentile specified)

There is a unit of measure for every statistic such as bytes, seconds, percent, and so on. While creating a custom metric, you need to define a unit, as if it is undefined, AWS CloudWatch uses none for that metric. Each statistic is available for a specified period of time that is cumulative metrics data collected for that period. Periods are defined in numbers of seconds such as 1, 5 or any multiple of 60. It can range from 1 second to one day, that is, 86,400 seconds, the default value is 60 seconds for a period. When you are specifying a statistic for a metric, you can define a start time, end time, and duration, for monitoring. The following figure shows the count of various metrics available for services that are used in my AWS account:

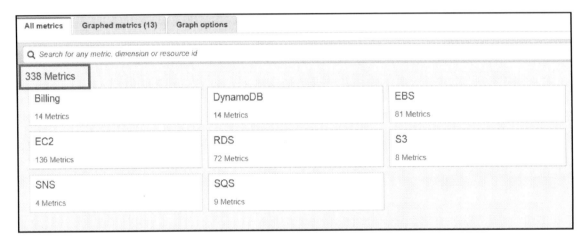

Figure 4 - AWS CloudWatch Metrics

Alarms allow us to automatically initiate an action on the user's behalf. These are performed on a single metric when the value of that metric crosses a threshold over a period of time. Alarms can be added to the dashboard.

The following figure shows details available for all metrics, such as the metric name, label, period, statistic, and so on. We can configure these metric details as per our requirements. On the right-hand side in the figure, you see the **Actions** tab; we can use this tab to configure actions such as alarms and notifications for our metrics:

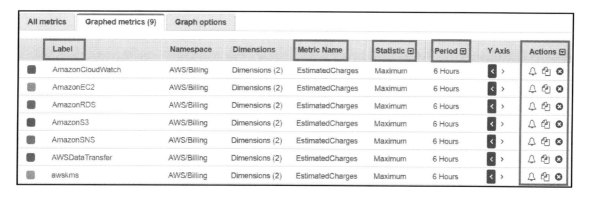

Figure 5 - AWS CloudWatch Metric details

Dashboards

Dashboards are web pages available in the AWS console that can be customized with metrics information in the form of graphs. These dashboards auto refresh when they are open and they can be shared with other users with appropriate permissions. Dashboards provide a unique place to have a consolidated view of all metrics and alarms available for all resources, such as AWS resources, or your applications located in all regions of an AWS account. All dashboards are global in nature, they are not region specific. You can create a dashboard using the AWS console, command-line tools or through the `PutDashboard` API.

You can use dashboards to monitor critical resources and applications on a real-time basis. You can have more than one dashboard; these can be saved and edited to add one or more metrics, graphs, widgets, texts such as links, comments, and so on. You can create up to 500 dashboards in your AWS account. An alarm can be added to a dashboard as well; this alarm will turn red when it is in a state of `ALARM`, that is, when it crosses the threshold set for the metric to trigger the alarm.

For adding metrics from multiple AWS regions to a single dashboard, perform the following steps as listed:

1. Navigate to the CloudWatch console through the AWS Management Console.
2. Click on **Metrics** in the navigation pane.
3. Choose the desired region in the navigation bar.
4. Select the metrics from this region.
5. Add them to the dashboard by clicking **Add to Dashboard** under **Actions**.

6. You can either add them to an existing dashboard or create a new dashboard.
7. For adding more metrics from different regions, repeat the above mentioned process.
8. Click on **Save Dashboard** to save this dashboard.

Let us also look at steps to create a dashboard through AWS Management Console:

1. Navigate to the CloudWatch console through the AWS Management Console.
2. Click on **Create Dashboard** in the navigation pane after choosing **Dashboards**.
3. Type the name of your dashboard and click on **Create Dashboard**.
4. You can add one of four options, **Line**, **Stacked area**, **Number**, or **Text** to your dashboard, as shown in the next screenshot.
5. You can add multiple widgets to your dashboard by following a similar process.
6. Once you have added all the required information to your dashboard, click on **Save Dashboard**.

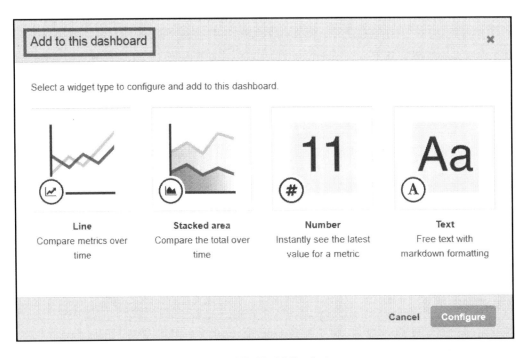

Figure 6 - AWS CloudWatch dashboard options

You can configure the refresh interval for your CloudWatch dashboards, ranging from 10 seconds to 15 minutes. You can also configure the auto refresh option for all your dashboards. Moreover, you can select a pre-defined time range for your dashboard, beginning from 1 hour and going up to 1 week. There is an option to have a customized time range, as well, for your dashboards.

Events

AWS CloudWatch Events is another useful component that provides a continuous stream of the state of all AWS resources whenever there is a change. These are system events that complement metrics and logs to provide a comprehensive picture of the overall health and state of your AWS resources and applications. AWS CloudWatch events help you to respond to changes to your resources, thereby making it a very useful tool for automating your responses in the event of a security threat. So, when your AWS resource or application changes their state, they will automatically send events to the AWS CloudWatch events stream. You will write a rule to be associated with these events and send these events to their targets to be processed, or you can take action on these events. You can also write rules to take action on a pre-configured schedule. For example, you can write a rule to take a snapshot of an Elastic Block Store volume at a pre-defined time. This lifecycle of events is depicted in the next diagram:

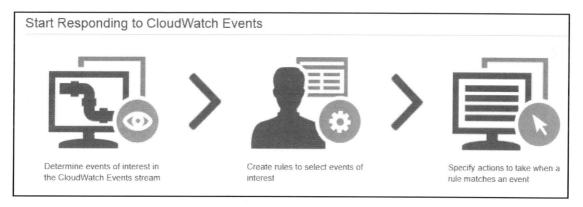

Figure 7 - AWS CloudWatch Events

AWS services such as AWS EC2, auto scaling, and CloudTrail emit events that are visible in AWS CloudWatch events. You can also generate custom events for your application using the PutEvents API. Targets are systems that process events. These targets could be an EC2 instance, a Lambda function, Kinesis streams, or your built-in targets. A target receives an event in the **JavaScript Object Notation (JSON)** format.

A rule will match events in a CloudWatch stream and route these events to targets for further processing. You can use a single rule to route to multiple targets; up to a maximum of 5 targets can be routed, and these can be processed in parallel. Rules are not sequential, that is, they are not processed in any particular order, allowing all departments in an organization to search and process events that are of interest to them. You can create a maximum of 100 rules per region for your AWS account. This is a soft limit and can be increased if required by contacting AWS support.

Alarms

An alarm watches over a single metric. You can create an alarm for any AWS resource you monitor, for example. you can monitor EC2 instances, S3 buckets, S3, billing, EBS volumes, databases, and so on. You can also create an alarm for a custom metric that you create for your application. An alarm will take one or more actions based on that metric crossing the threshold either once or multiple times over a period of time. These actions could be one of the following:

- EC2 action
- Auto scaling
- Notification to an SNS topic

You can add alarms to dashboards. You can also view alarm history for the past 14 days, either through the AWS CloudWatch console or through the API by using the `DescribeAlarmHistory` function. There are three states of an alarm, as follows:

- `OK`: Metric is within the defined threshold
- `ALARM`: Metric has breached the threshold
- `INSUFFICIENT_DATA`: Either the metric is not available or there isn't enough metric data available to evaluate the state of the alarm

You can create a maximum of 5000 alarms in every region in your AWS account. You can create alarms for various functions such as starting, stopping, terminating, or recovering an EC2 instance in the event of an incident, or when an instance is undergoing an interruption in service.

There are two steps for creating an alarm; first we need to select a metric and second we need to define an alarm. We have already looked at step 2 earlier in this chapter. Let us look at step one, **1. Select Metric**, as shown in the following figure.

The following example is for creating an alarm for a stand alone EC2 instance. Note that we can also create alarms for an auto scaling group, an **Amazon Machine Image (AMI)**, or across all instances. We selected CPUUtilization metric, among one of many metrics available for an EC2 instance. Statistic chosen is **Average** and the period is **5 Minutes**:

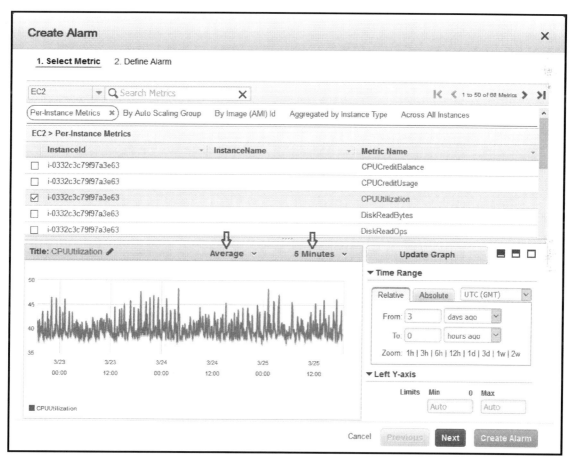

Figure 8 - AWS CloudWatch alarm

Log Monitoring

AWS CloudWatch Logs enable you to monitor and store logs from various sources such as EC2 logs, CloudTrail logs, logs for Lambda functions, and so on. You can create metric filters for these log data and treat them in similar way as any other metrics. You can create alarms for these metrics, add them to dashboards, and take actions against these alarms. It uses your log data to monitor, so it does not require any code changes. Your log data is encrypted while in transit and at rest when it is processed by AWS CloudWatch Logs. You can consume log data from resources in any region, however, you can view log data only through AWS CloudWatch Logs in regions where this is supported.

AWS CloudWatch Logs is a fully managed service so you don't have to worry about managing the infrastructure to support an increase in your load when you have scores of resources sending continuous log streams to CloudWatch Logs for storage, processing, and monitoring.

As shown in the next figure, we have created a graph called `LambdaLog` that shows log group metrics such as `IncomingLogEvents` and `IncomingBytes`. These metrics can be monitored for multiple log groups. Moreover, these logs can be shared through the AWS CloudWatch console. Just like any other graph in AWS CloudWatch, we have an option to select a period and graph type. For this example, we chose the graph 1 week of data in the **Stacked area** format:

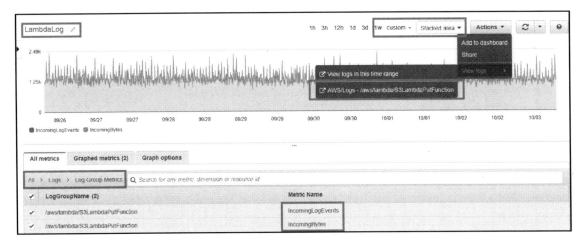

Figure 9 - AWS CloudWatch log monitoring

To create a logs metric filter, you need to follow a two step process: first you define a pattern and then you assign a metric. By creating these metric filters, we can monitor events in a log group as and when they are sent to CloudWatch Logs. We can monitor and count exact values such as `Error` or `404` from these log events and use this information to take any actions.

For the first step, we need to create a logs metric filter as shown in the next screenshot. In this example, we are searching for the `Error` word in our log data to find out how many errors we have received for our Lambda function. This Lambda function, `S3LambdaPutFunction`, is sending continuous log streams to the CloudWatch Logs. You can also test this metric filter based on your existing log data.

Once you are done with this step, you can go to the second step and assign values for your metric such as metric name, metric value, and metric namespace:

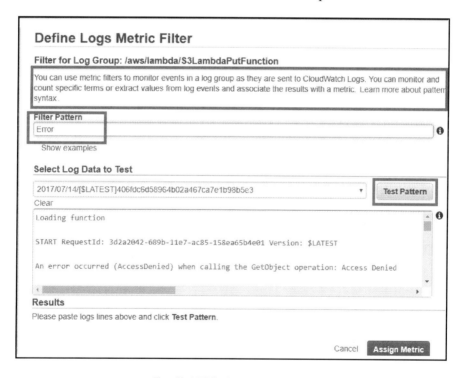

Figure 10 - AWS CloudWatch Create Logs Metric

Monitoring Amazon EC2

For all your servers in the cloud that you provision through the Amazon **Elastic Compute Cloud (EC2)** service, monitoring is an integral part for maintaining security, availability, and an acceptable level of performance for these servers, as well as applications running on those servers. AWS provides multiple manuals as well as automated solutions for monitoring your EC2 instances comprehensively. AWS recommends having a monitoring plan in place to effectively monitor your EC2 instances so that you can have reactive as well as proactive measures in place in the event of an incident.

A typical monitoring plan contains the following information:

- Identify resources to be monitored
- Define tools for monitoring these resources
- Choose metrics to be monitored for these resources
- Define thresholds for these metrics
- Set alarms for these thresholds with actions
- Identify users to be notified through these alarms
- Configure actions to be taken in the state of alarm

Once you have a monitoring plan in place, setup a baseline for acceptable performance of your EC2 instances and applications. This baseline would consist of metrics such as CPU utilization, disk usage, memory utilization, network performance, and so on. You should continuously measure your monitoring plan against this baseline performance and update your plan if required.

Automated monitoring tools

Let us look at automated monitoring tools available in AWS to monitor your EC2 instances:

System status checks: AWS continuously monitors the status of AWS resources that are required to keep your EC2 instances up and running. If a problem is found, it will require AWS involvement to get fixed. You have an option to wait for AWS to fix this problem or you can resolve it yourself either by stopping, terminating, replacing, or restarting an instance. The following are the common reasons for system status check failure:

- Hardware and/or software issues on the system host
- Loss of power on the system
- Loss of network connectivity

Instance status checks: AWS also continuously checks the software and network configuration for all of your instances that might result in the degradation of performance of your EC2 instances. Usually, you will be required to fix such issues by either restarting your instance or making changes in the operating system for your instance. The following are the common reasons for instance status check failure:

- Corrupt filesystem
- Failed system status check
- Exhausted memory
- Issues with networking configuration
- Incompatible Kernel

The following screenshot shows a successfully completed system status checks and instance status checks for one instance in the AWS console:

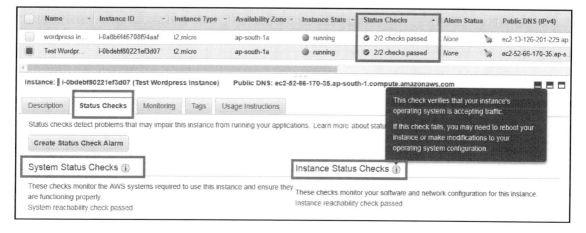

Figure 11 - AWS system and instance checks

- **CloudWatch alarms**: You can configure alarms for sustained state changes for your resources for a configurable period or a number of periods. You can watch a metric for your instance and take multiple actions such as sending a notification or trigger to the auto scaling policy based on CloudWatch alarms. Note that alarms work when there is a sustained change in the state of resources; they don't work when the state is changed once.

- **CloudWatch events**: You can automate responses to system events for all your AWS services and resources by using CloudWatch events. System events or custom events for your resources are delivered to the CloudWatch events stream on a near real-time basis, which enables you to take action immediately. You can write rules for system events as soon as they reach the CloudWatch events stream. These rules can contain automated actions in response to system events.
- **CloudWatch logs**: You can monitor, store, and process logs from your EC2 instances using CloudWatch logs. This is a fully managed service, so you don't have to worry about managing the infrastructure for log management for your EC2 instances.
- **EC2 monitoring scripts**: You can write scripts in Perl or Python to monitor your EC2 instances through custom metrics that are not natively provided by AWS CloudWatch. Some of these metrics are memory, disk, and so on, and are not available in AWS CloudWatch because AWS does not have access to the operating systems of your EC2 instance.
- **AWS Management Pack for Microsoft System Center Operations Manager**: You can link your EC2 instances with operating systems such as Linux or Windows running inside these EC2 instances with the help of this pack. It is an extension to the existing Microsoft System Center Operations Manager. You can access and monitor applications running on your AWS resources with the help of this AWS Management Pack and gain deep insights about the health and performance of these applications. This pack uses metrics and alarms to monitor your AWS resources in AWS CloudWatch. These metrics and alarms appear as performance counters and alerts in the Microsoft System Center.

    By using this pack, which is available in the form of a plug in, you can view all your resources in a single Operations Manager console. You need to download and install it to use it.

You can monitor the following AWS resources, among many others that are shown in the following figure:

- EC2 instances
- EBS volumes
- CloudWatch alarms
- CloudWatch custom alerts
- CloudFormation stacks
- Elastic beanstalk applications

The AWS Management Pack for System Center 2012 Operations Manager can discover and monitor your AWS resources, such as EC2 instances, Elastic Load Balancers, and so on, by using management servers that are part of a resource pool. This pool can get additional capacity by adding more management servers if the number of AWS resources to be monitored is increased.

A typical AWS Management Pack has multiple components as shown in the following figure:

- **Operations manager infrastructure**: This consists of management servers, one or multiple servers that can be deployed either on-premises or in AWS. This infrastructure also includes dependencies for these servers including Microsoft SQL Server and so on.
- **Resource pool**: This pool consists of one or more management server that have internet connectivity for communicating with AWS through AWS SDK for .NET.
- **AWS credentials**: These credentials include an access key ID along with a secret access key. These credentials are passed in API calls to AWS by management servers. AWS Management Pack needs to be configured with these credentials. AWS recommends that an IAM user with read-only access is created along with these credentials.

- **EC2 instances**: You will install an operations manager agent on these EC2 instances in order to see the operating system and application metrics along with EC2 instance metrics. These are virtual computers in the AWS cloud.

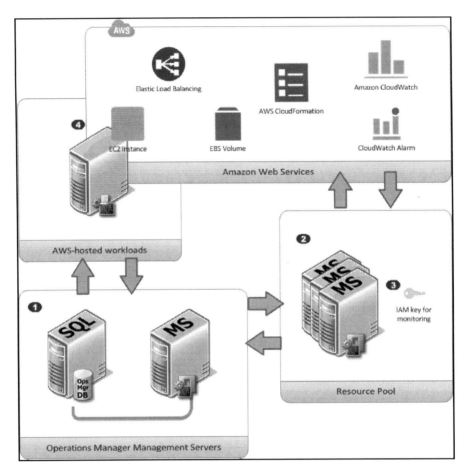

Figure 12 - AWS Management Pack

Manual monitoring tools

While AWS provides multiple tools, services, and solutions to automate monitoring for your EC2 instances, there are data points and items that are not covered by these automated monitoring tools. For such items, we need to rely on EC2 dashboards and CloudWatch dashboards available in the AWS Management Console. Let us look at these two dashboards:

- **EC2 dashboard**: The EC2 dashboard shows the following information about your EC2 instances and the environment in which your EC2 instances are running:
    - Service health and scheduled events for the selected region
    - Instance state
    - Status checks
    - Alarm status
    - Metric details for instances
    - Metric details for volumes
- **CloudWatch dashboard**: You can use the CloudWatch dashboard to troubleshoot issues related to EC2 instances and monitor the metrics trends. These trends can be analyzed to provide insights about health and performance of your AWS resources including your EC2 instances. You can search and plot metrics on graphs for your EC2 instances. Alongside this, you can also see the following information on the CloudWatch dashboard:
    - Current alarms and their status
    - Graphs of alarms and resources
    - Service health status

Best practices for monitoring EC2 instances

Let us look at the following best practices for monitoring EC2 instances:

- Ensure monitoring is prioritized for hiving off small issues before they become big problems; use the drill down approach
- Create and implement a comprehensive monitoring plan as discussed earlier in this chapter
- Use AWS CloudWatch to collect, monitor, and analyze data for all your resources in all regions
- Automate monitoring of all your resources
- Continuously monitor and check log files for your EC2 instances
- Periodically review your alarms and thresholds
- Use one monitoring platform to monitor all your AWS resources and applications running on these AWS resources
- Integrate metrics, logs, alarms, and trends to get a complete picture of your entire environment

Summary

In this chapter, we learnt about monitoring the cloud and how AWS CloudWatch enables us to monitor all resources in AWS cloud through its various features, and the benefits of using AWS CloudWatch. We also went through its architecture in detail.

We learnt about all the components of AWS CloudWatch such as metrics, alarms, dashboards, and so on, to create a comprehensive monitoring solution for our workload. We now know how to monitor predefined and custom metrics as well as how to log data from multiple sources, such as EC2 instances, applications, AWS CloudTrail, and so on.

Next, we learnt about monitoring EC2 instances for our servers in the cloud. We went through various automated and manual tools available in AWS to monitor our EC2 instances thoroughly. We deep dived into AWS Management Pack, which helps us to monitor all our resources in AWS and outside of AWS in one common console.

Lastly, we learnt about the best practices for monitoring EC2 instances.

In the next chapter, *Logging and Auditing in AWS*, we will learn how logging and auditing works in AWS. These two activities go hand in hand for any environment, and AWS ensures that its users have all the information they require when it comes to logging and auditing. Most of the AWS service generates logs for all activities, and AWS has one fully managed service in AWS CloudTrail that logs all API activities for your AWS account.

We will learn about these AWS services, and we will also learn about creating a fully managed logging and auditing solution, in the next chapter.

8

Logging and Auditing in AWS

Logging and auditing are required for any organization from a compliance and governance point of view. If your organization operates in one of the highly regulated industries such as banking, financial services, healthcare, and so on, then it must go through frequent security audits in order to maintain compliance with industry regulations. These audits can be internal or external depending on the nature of your business.

We learnt in the previous chapters that security of the IT environment is a shared responsibility between AWS and its customers. While AWS is responsible for maintaining security of resources, tools, services, and features available in the AWS cloud, the customer is responsible for configuring security for all these services and the security of their data. AWS communicates information related to security with customers periodically by taking the following steps:

- Obtaining industry standard certifications
- By third party audits and attestations
- Publishing white papers and content about the security infrastructure
- Providing audit certifications and other regulatory compliance documents to customers

Logging refers to recording activities for your resources. A log data from your resource is required to understand the state of your resource at a given point in time and also for communications and data transfer to and from your resource. Logging also enables you to diagnose and mitigate any issue either reported, discovered, or expected for a resource or multiple resources in your system. This logged data is generally stored in a separate storage device and is used for auditing, forensics, and compliance purposes as well. Logged data is often used long after the resource that generated the log data is terminated. Logging is a reactive security measure.

Each AWS service provides log data in the form of log files, this data is used to get information about the performance of this service. Moreover, many AWS services provide security log data that has information about access, billing, configuration changes, and so on. These log files are used for auditing, governance, compliance, risk management, and so on.

AWS provides you with a fully managed service AWS CloudTrail to log and audit all activities in your account. This includes operational auditing and risk auditing as well. Furthermore, you can use AWS-managed services such as Amazon S3, Amazon CloudWatch, Amazon ElasticSearch, and so on to create a centralized logging solution to get a comprehensive view of your IT environment, including all resources, applications, and users.

AWS has one the most effective and longest running customer compliance program available today in the cloud market. AWS enables its customers and partners to manage security controls in the cloud with the help of compliance tooling's largest and most diverse compliance footprint. All these features together allow; AWS customers and partners to work with their auditors by providing all the evidence required for effective control of IT operations and security and data protection in the cloud.

A secured cloud environment is a compliant cloud environment. AWS offers you a cloud-based governance for your environment with a number of advantages, such as a lower cost of entry, configurable and secure operations, agility, a holistic view of your entire IT environment, security controls, governance enabled features, and central automation. While using AWS, you inherit all the security controls operated by AWS, thereby reducing your overhead on deploying and maintaining these security controls yourselves.

In this chapter, we will learn about logging, auditing, risks, and governance in the AWS cloud and how they are integrated with each other. We will begin with understanding logging in AWS, how logging works for various AWS services in AWS and what tools and services are available to work with log data of different shapes and sizes generated from a myriad of resources in your IT environment. While going through logging, we'll learn about the following:

- AWS native security logging capabilities
- AWS CloudWatch Logs

Next, we will learn about AWS CloudTrail, a fully managed audit service that logs all API activities in your AWS account. This service is at the heart of governance, logging, and auditing in AWS along with AWS CloudWatch Logs. It also helps with compliance and risk monitoring activities. We will learn about CloudTrail concepts before moving on to deep dive in to features and use cases of AWS CloudTrail. Moreover, we will learn how to have security at scale through logging in AWS and best practices for AWS CloudTrail.

Moving on, we will walk through auditing in AWS. We will walk through the following resources provided by AWS:

- AWS Compliance Center
- AWS Auditor Learning Path

AWS has many resources to audit usage of AWS services. We will walk through a fully managed service AWS Artifact to obtain all security and compliance related documents. Furthermore, we will learn how we can use the following AWS services for risk, compliance, and governance in the AWS cloud in a variety of ways:

- AWS Config
- AWS Service Catalog
- AWS Trusted Advisor

We will wrap up the auditing section by going through the following auditing checklist and learning about other available resources for auditing AWS resources:

- AWS auditing security checklist

Logging in AWS

AWS has a complete suite of services to cater to all your logging needs for adhering to your security and operational best practices, as well as meeting your compliance and regulatory requirements. So, you have all the logs that you need to capture, with storage, monitoring, and analyzing facilities available in AWS, keeping the dynamic nature of cloud computing.

To begin, let us look at various logs available in AWS. All the logs in AWS can be classified into three categories, as shown in the following table:

AWS infrastructure logs	AWS service logs	Host-based logs
AWS CloudTrail	Amazon S3	Messages
AWS VPC flow logs	AWS ELB	IIS/Apache
	Amazon CloudFront	Windows Event logs
	AWS Lambda	Custom logs

Table 1 - AWS logs classification

AWS infrastructure logs, such as CloudTrail Logs, contain information related to all API activity in your AWS account, while VPC flow logs contain information regarding your IP traffic flowing in and out of your VPC.

AWS service logs include logs from miscellaneous AWS services that contain information such as security log data, service access information, changes related to configuration and state, billing events, and so on.

Host-based logs are generated by the operating system of EC2 instances, such as Apache, IIS, and so on. Applications running on AWS services or custom logs are generated by web servers.

All of these logs generated by various sources will have a different format, size, frequency, and information. AWS provides you with services and solutions to effectively manage, store, access, analyze, and monitor these logs.

AWS native security logging capabilities

Let us look at the best practices for working with log files and native AWS Security logging capabilities for some of the foundation and most common AWS services.

Best practices

Let us look at best practices for logging:

- You should always log access and audit information for all your resources
- Ensure that all your log data is secured with access control and stored in a durable storage solution such as S3, as shown in the following figure
- Use lifecycle policies to automate storage, archiving, and deletion of your log data
- Follow standard naming conventions for your log data
- Use centralized log monitoring solutions to consolidate all your log data from all sources, analyze it, and create actionable alerts out of this log data

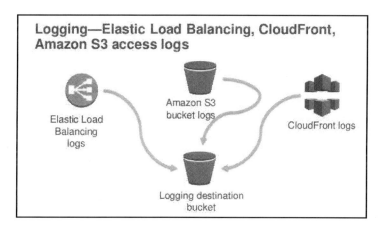

Figure 1 - AWS access logging S3

AWS CloudTrail

AWS CloudTrail is an audit service that records all API calls made to your AWS account. You can use this log data to track user activity and API usage in your AWS account. This service should be enabled for your AWS account to collect data for all regions irrespective of the location of your resources. This service stores historical data for the last seven days, you need to store this data in an S3 bucket in order to store it for a longer duration. This service integrates seamlessly with AWS CloudWatch Logs and AWS Lambda to create a log monitoring and processing solution. We will deep dive into AWS CloudTrail later in this chapter.

AWS Config

AWS Config service records the configurations of all AWS resources in your AWS account. It is used to audit changes to the resource configuration as it provides a timeline of such changes for specific AWS services. It uses S3 to store snapshots of all such changes so that your data is stored securely in a durable, access controlled storage. AWS Config integrates with **Simple Notification Service** (**SNS**) to configure the notification to users when changes are made to a resource. This service enables you to demonstrate compliance at a given point in time or during a period. We will look at AWS Config in detail later in this chapter.

AWS detailed billing reports

You have the option, to break down your billing report by month, day, or by an hour; by a product, such as EC2, or by a resource, such as a specific EC2 instance or specific S3 bucket; or by tags assigned to your resources. These detailed billing reports are used to analyze usage and audit consumption of AWS resources in your account. These detailed billing reports are provided multiple times in a day to the S3 bucket of your choice. Always allocate meaningful tags for your resources to allocate the cost to these AWS resources based on their cost centers, departments, projects, and so on. Detailed billing reports help you improve cost analysis, resource optimization, and billing reconciliation processes.

Amazon S3 Access Logs

S3 logs all the requests made to individual S3 buckets when you have enabled the logging option for an S3 bucket. This access log stores all information about access requests, such as requester, bucket name, request time, error log, and so on. You can use this information for your security audits including failed access attempts for your S3 buckets. It will also help you understand the usage of objects in and across your S3 buckets and traffic patterns along with mapping your AWS S3 charges with S3 usage. We will look at server access logging for S3 buckets later in this section.

ELB Logs

ELB provides access logs with detailed information for all requests and connections sent to your load balancers. ELB publishes a log file in five minute intervals for every load balancer node once you enable this feature. This log file contains information such as client IP address, latency, server response, and so on. This information can be used for security and access analysis to ensure you are not getting traffic from unauthorized sources. You can also use latency and request time information to detect degradation in performance and take actions required to improve the user experience. Alternatively, these logs provide an external view of your application's performance. You can configure an S3 bucket to store these logs. The following figure shows the logging process for Amazon ELB:

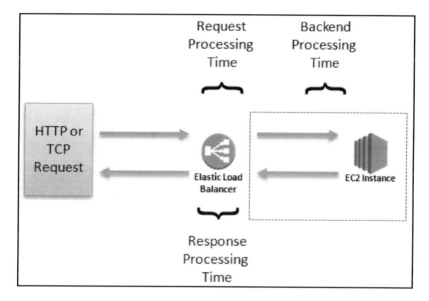

Figure 2 - Amazon ELB logging

Amazon CloudFront Access Logs

Amazon CloudFront can be configured to generate access logs. These logs are delivered multiple times an hour to an S3 bucket that you specify for saving this log data. These logs provide information about every user request made to CloudFront distributions just like S3 access logs and ELB access logs. Similarly, this log data can be used for security and access audits for all your users accessing content throughout your content delivery network. You can use this data to verify if your content delivery network is performing as per your expectation. You can check latency of content delivered along with delivery errors and take required actions based on log data. The following figure shows how logging works for Amazon CloudFront:

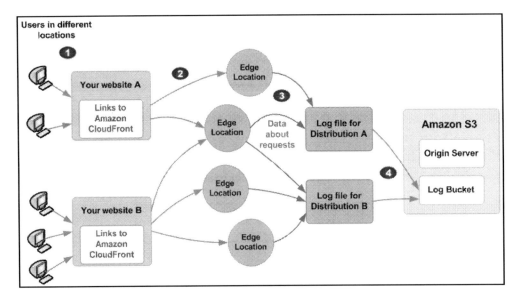

Figure 3 - Amazon CloudFront logging

Amazon RDS Logs

These logs store information such as performance, access, and errors for your RDS databases. You can view, download, and watch these logs from the AWS Management Console, CLI, or through Amazon RDS APIs. You can also query these log files through database tables specific to your database engine. You can use these log files for security, performance, access, and operational analysis of your managed database in RDS. You should have an automated process to transfer your log files to a centralized access log repository such as S3 or Amazon CloudWatch Logs.

Amazon VPC Flow Logs

VPC flow logs capture all information about all IP traffic flowing in and out of your VPC network interfaces. You can enable flow logs for a VPC, a subnet, or even at a single **Elastic Network Interface (ENI)**. This log data is stored and viewed in the CloudWatch Logs. It can also be exported for advanced analytics. This log data can be used for auditing, debugging, or when you are required to capture and analyze network flow data for security or regulatory purposes. You can troubleshoot all scenarios when your traffic is not reaching its expected destination with the help of VPC flow logs. The following figure shows VPC flow logs being published to the Amazon CloudWatch Logs to store log data in multiple log streams under one log group:

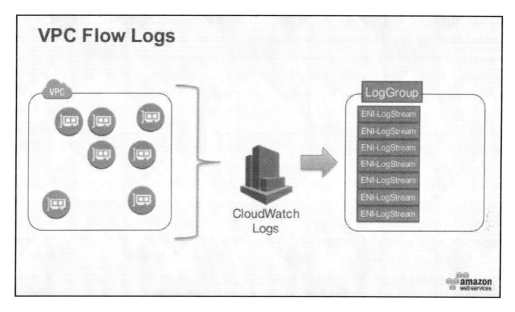

Figure 4 - Amazon VPC flow logs

AWS CloudWatch Logs

AWS CloudWatch Logs is a monitoring, logging, and log storage feature available as part of the AWS CloudWatch service. You can consume logs from resources in any AWS region; however, you can view logs in the CloudWatch for regions where CloudWatch Logs are supported. Your log data can be encrypted using KMS at the log group level. CloudWatch Logs are primarily used for performing the following tasks:

- Monitoring all your logs in near real-time by routing them to the AWS CloudWatch Logs; these could be your operating system logs, application logs, AWS service logs, or AWS infrastructure logs such as VPC flow logs and AWS CloudTrail Logs
- Storing all your logs in a durable storage with configurable retention period
- Generating logs for your EC2 instances by installing the CloudWatch Logs agent on your EC2 instances
- Integrated with AWS services such as AWS CloudWatch for creating metrics and alerts, AWS IAM for secure access to logs and AWS CloudTrail for recording all API activities for AWS CloudWatch Logs in your AWS account

CloudWatch Logs concepts

Let us now look at the following core concepts of AWS CloudWatch Logs to understand it better:

- **Log events**: Records of any activity captured by the application or resource that is being logged. A log event contains the timestamp and event message in UTF-8 format.
- **Log streams**: A sequence of log events from the same source being logged such as an application or an EC2 instance.
- **Log group**: A group of multiple log streams that share the same properties such as retention period, policies, access control, and so on. Each log stream is part of a log group. These log groups can be tagged as well.

- **Metric filters**: A metric filter is used to extract metrics out of the log data that is ingested by the CloudWatch Logs. A metric filter is assigned to a log group, and this filter is assigned to all log streams of that log group. You can have more than one metric filter for a log group.

- **Retention policies**: You define retention policies for storing your log data in CloudWatch Logs. These policies are assigned to log groups and log streams belonging to that log group. Log data is automatically deleted once it is expired. By default, log data is stored indefinitely. You can set up a retention period of 1 day to 10 years.

- **Log agent**: You need to install a CloudWatch log agent in your EC2 instances to send log data to CloudWatch Logs automatically. An agent contains the following components:
  - A plug-in to CLI to push log data to CloudWatch Logs
  - A script to start pushing data to CloudWatch Logs
  - A cron job to check that script is running as per schedule

The following figure shows four log groups available under CloudWatch Logs in the AWS CloudWatch console. It also shows **Metric Filters** available for one of the log groups containing **2 filters**. Moreover, it shows that retention policies are not set up for any log group, hence log events are set to **Never Expire**:

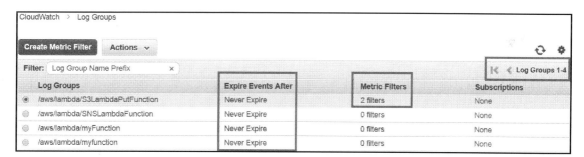

Figure 5 - AWS CloudWatch Logs

The following figure shows log streams for a log group in the AWS CloudWatch console. You can filter log streams based on text data. You can also create a custom log stream and you also have an option to delete log streams:

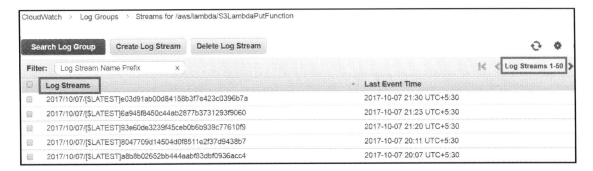

Figure 6 - AWS CloudWatch Log streams

The following figure shows event logs for a log stream in a log group. You can filter events based on text or phrases such as error or access denied. Note that events contain such information along with a timestamp, as shown in the following figure. You can view information for the past 30 seconds up to the time when the event was first logged, as shown in the following figure:

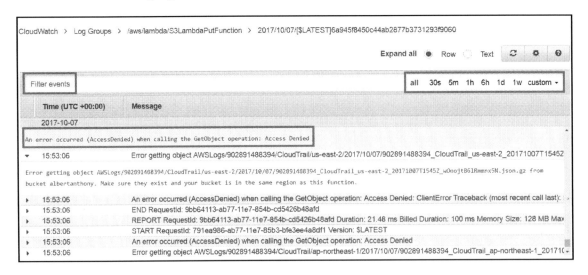

Figure 7 - AWS CloudWatch events log

CloudWatch Logs limits

Let us look at limits of CloudWatch Logs:

- A batch can have a maximum size of 1 MB
- 5 GB of data archiving is free
- An event can have a maximum size of 256 KB
- You can get 10 requests for log events per second, per account, per region
- 5 GB of incoming data is free
- You can have up to 5,000 log groups per account, per region. This is a soft limit and can be increased by contacting AWS support
- You can have up to 100 metric filters for every log group
- You can have one subscription filter per log group

Lifecycle of CloudWatch Logs

A typical CloudWatch Logs lifecycle begins by installing a log agent on an EC2 instance. This agent will publish data to the CloudWatch Logs, where it will be part of a log stream in a log group. This log stream will process events data using filters and metrics will be created for this log data. Additionally, this log group can have subscriptions to process this log data in real time.

The following figure shows the lifecycle where logs are published by the CloudWatch Log agent to the CloudWatch Logs from various EC2 instances inside a VPC. Log agent is installed in all these EC2 instances. CloudWatch Logs will process these multiple logs and create CloudWatch metrics, alarms, and notifications for these logs:

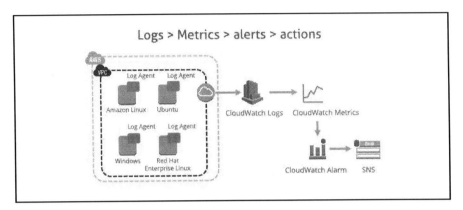

Figure 8 - AWS CloudWatch Log agent lifecycle

Alternatively, CloudWatch Logs will have one or multiple logs published by various other sources apart from the CloudWatch Log agent, such as AWS Lambda, Elastic Load Balancer, S3 buckets and so on. It will monitor, process, and store all such logs in a similar fashion as previously described.

Following figure shows logs from the ELB stored in the S3 bucket. Whenever a log arrives from the ELB in the S3 bucket, this buckets sends an event notification that invokes an AWS Lambda function. This AWS Lambda function reads this log data and publishes it to the CloudWatch Logs for further processing:

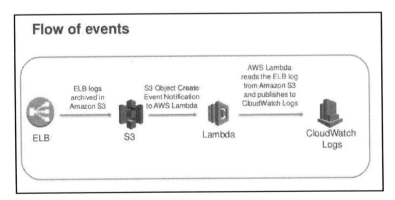

Figure 9 - AWS CloudWatch Logs lifecycle

AWS CloudTrail

AWS CloudTrail is a fully managed audit service that captures all API activities in the form of event history in your AWS account for all resources. Simply put, all actions performed by a user, role, or an AWS service are recorded as events by this service. This includes API calls made from the AWS Management Console, CLI tools, SDKs, APIs, and other AWS services. It stores this information in log files. These logs files can be delivered to S3 for durable storage. AWS CloudTrail enables compliance, governance, risk auditing, and operational auditing of your AWS account. This event history is used for security analysis, tracking changes for your resources, analyzing user activity, demonstrating compliance, and various other scenarios that require visibility in your account activities.

AWS CloudTrail is enabled by default for all AWS accounts. It shows seven days of event history by default for the current region that you are viewing. In order to view the event history for more than seven days for all the AWS regions, you need to enable and set up a CloudTrail. You can view, search, and download this event data for further analysis. These log files are encrypted by default. These log files are delivered within 15 minutes of any activity occurring in your AWS account. They are published by AWS CloudTrail approximately every five minutes.

The following flow diagram shows typical lifecycle for CloudTrail events in five steps:

1. Account activity occurs.
2. This activity is captured by CloudTrail in the form of a CloudTrail event.
3. This event history is available for viewing and downloading.
4. You can configure an S3 bucket for storing the CloudTrail event history.
5. CloudTrail will send event logs to the S3 bucket and optionally publish them to CloudWatch Logs and CloudWatch events as well.

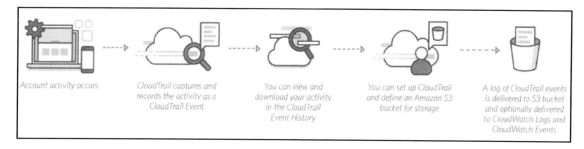

Figure 10 - AWS CloudTrail lifecycle

AWS CloudTrail concepts

- **CloudTrail events**: A record of an activity or an action captured by CloudTrail in an AWS account. This action can be performed by a user, a role, or any AWS service that is integrated with CloudTrail for recording events. These events allow you to get the history of API as well as non-API activities for your AWS account for all actions performed through the AWS Management Console, CLIs, AWS SDKs, and APIs.
- **CloudTrail event history**: You get event details for the past seven days by default. You can view, search, and download these details through CLIs or through the AWS Management Console for your consumption. This history data provides insight into activities and actions taken by your users or applications on your AWS resources and services.
- **Trails**: You use trails to ensure your CloudTrail events are sent either to a pre-defined S3 bucket, CloudWatch Logs, or CloudWatch events. It is a configurable item to filter and deliver your events to multiple sources for storage, monitoring, and further processing. It is also used to encrypt your CloudTrail event log files using AWS KMS along with setting up notifications using the Amazon SNS for delivery of event log files. You can create up to five trails in a region.
- **Accessing and managing CloudTrail**: You can access and manage CloudTrail through AWS Management Console. This console provides a user interface for CloudTrail for performing the most common tasks such as :
    - Viewing event logs and event history
    - Searching and downloading event details
    - Creating a trail or editing one
    - Configuring trails for storage, notification, encryption, or monitoring

Alternatively, you can also use CLIs, CloudTrail APIs, and AWS SDKs to programmatically access and manage AWS CloudTrail.

- **Access control**: CloudTrail is integrated with IAM, so you can control users and permissions for accessing CloudTrail in your AWS account. Follow IAM best practices for granting access and do not share credentials. Use roles instead of users for all programmatic access and revoke access if service is not accessed for a while.

AWS CloudTrail benefits

- **Simplified compliance**: You can use AWS CloudTrail for simplifying compliance audits for internal policies and regulatory standards. AWS CloudTrail supports automation of event log storage and recording for all activities in your AWS account. It also integrates seamlessly with AWS CloudWatch Logs that allows you to search log data, create metric filters for any events that are not following compliance policies, raise alarms, and send notifications. This automation and integration enables quicker resolution for investigating incidents and faster responses to auditor requests with the required data.

- **User and resource activity visibility**: AWS CloudTrail enables you to gain visibility into user and resource activity for your AWS account by capturing every single API call, including login to AWS Management Console as well. For every call it captures, it records information such as who made the call, the IP address of the source, what service was called, the time of the call, what action was performed, the response by the AWS resource and so on.

- **Security analysis and troubleshooting**: Using information collected by AWS CloudTrail, you can troubleshoot incidents in your AWS account quickly and more accurately. You can also precisely discover operational issues by searching filtering events for a specific period.

- **Security automation**: Using AWS CloudTrail event logs, you can automate your security responses for events and incidents threatening security of your application and resources in your AWS account. This automation is enabled by AWS CloudTrail integration with AWS CloudWatch events that helps you to define fully automated workflows for security vulnerabilities detection and remediation. For example, you can create a workflow that encrypts an **Elastic Block Storage (EBS)** volume as soon as a CloudTrail event detects that is was un-encrypted.

A CloudTrail event captures the following information about an event, as shown in the following figure:

- **Event time**
- **User name**
- **Event name**
- **Resource type**
- **AWS access key**

- **Event source**
- **AWS region**
- **Error code**
- **Request ID**
- **Event ID**
- **Source IP address**
- **Resources Referenced**

The following figure shows a couple of events in the CloudTrail event log. You can see the user name, such as `root` and `S3LambdaPutFunction`:

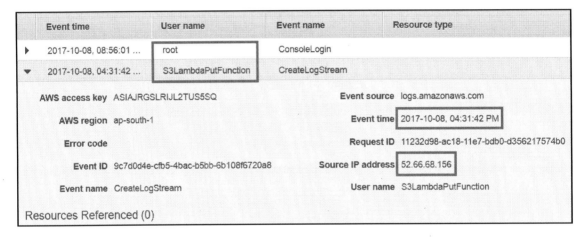

Figure 11 - AWS CloudTrail events

AWS CloudTrail use cases

- **Compliance aid**: Uses the history of all activities to verify if your environment was compliant at a given period in time. IT auditors can use AWS CloudTrail event log files as a compliance aid. The following figure depicts a typical workflow for a compliance audit activity that includes AWS resource modifications log, verification of log integrity, and log review for unauthorized access:

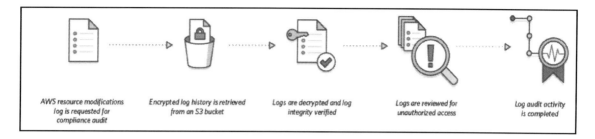

Figure 12 - AWS CloudTrail compliance audit workflow

- **Security analysis and automation**: IT and security administrators can perform security analysis and automate the response by analyzing user behavior and patterns present in log files. The following figure shows a workflow for one such scenario. A trail is a setup for logging user activity. These logs are ingested into a log management, and analytics system for analyzing user behavior for any suspicious activity. An automated action can neutralize a security threat based on analysis since logs are delivered in near real-time:

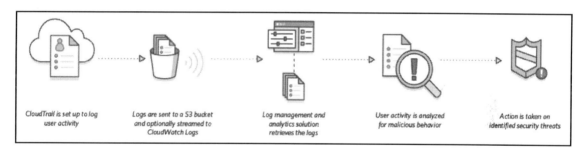

Figure 13 - AWS CloudTrail security analysis workflow

- **Data exfiltration**: You can also detect unauthorized data transfer for any of your resources in your AWS account through the CloudTrail event history. The following figure depicts a workflow for detecting one such activity based on a data event log stored in the S3 bucket. Once this suspicious activity is detected, the security team is notified for further investigation and actions:

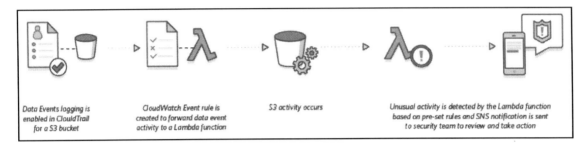

Figure 14 - AWS CloudTrail data exfiltration workflow

- **Operational issue troubleshooting**: DevOps engineers and IT administrators can track changes and resolve operational issues by using API call history available in the AWS CloudTrail. This history includes details of creation, modification, deletion of all your AWS resources such as security groups, EC2 instances, S3 buckets, and so on. The following figure shows an example of an operational issue caused by a change to an AWS resource. This change can be detected by filtering CloudTrail API activity history for this resource name, such as the name of the EC2 instance. Once the change is identified, it can either be rolled back or corrective actions can be taken to resolve operational issues related to this EC2 instance:

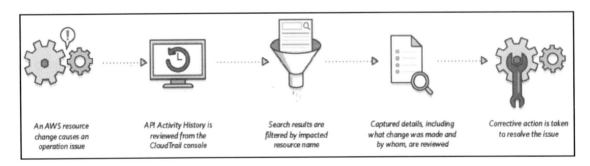

Figure 15 - AWS CloudTrail operational issue troubleshooting workflow

Security at Scale with AWS Logging

Logging and monitoring of API calls are considered best practices for security and operational control. These are also often required by industry regulators and compliance auditors for organizations operating in highly regulated domains such as finance, healthcare, and so on. AWS CloudTrail is a web service that logs all API calls in your AWS environment. In this section, we are going to learn about the following five common requirements for compliance around logging and how AWS CloudTrail satisfies these requirements. These five requirements are extracted from the common compliance frameworks, such as PCI DSS v2.0, FEDRAMP, ISO 27001:2005, and presented in the form of controls and logging domains:

- **Control access to log files**: One of the primary logging requirements is to ensure that access to log files is controlled. AWS CloudTrail integrates with AWS IAM to control access to log files. Log files that are stored in S3 buckets have access control in the form of bucket policies, access control lists as well as **multi-factor authentication (MFA)** for secured access. You can control unauthorized access to this service and provide granular read and write access to log files through various features available in AWS.

- **Receive alerts on log file creation and misconfiguration**: A logging service should send alerts whenever a log file is created or if it fails to create a log due to an incorrect configuration. When AWS CloudTrail delivers log files to S3 buckets or to CloudWatch Logs, event notifications can be configured to notify users about new log files. Similarly, when a log file fails to generate, AWS CloudTrail can send notifications through SNS in the AWS Management Console.

- **Manage changes to AWS resources and log files**: One of the primary requirements for many compliance audits is providing change logs for all resources for addition, deletion, and modification along with security of this change log itself. AWS CloudTrail stores change logs by capturing system change events for all AWS resources for any change in the state by API calls made through AWS Management Console, AWS SDKs, APIs, or CLIs. This API call log file is stored in S3 buckets in an encrypted format. It can be further secured by enabling MFA and using IAM to grant read-only access for these S3 buckets.

- **Storage of log files**: Many regulatory compliance programs and industry standards require you to store your log files for varying periods ranging from a year to many years. For example, PCI DSS compliance requires that log files are stored for one year; HIPPA compliance requires that log data is stored for a period of six years. AWS CloudTrail seamlessly integrates with S3 to provide you secure, durable, highly available, and scalable storage without any administrative overhead. Moreover, you can set up lifecycle policies in S3 to transition data to the Amazon Glacier for archival purposes, while maintaining durability, security, and resiliency of your log data. By default, logs are set for an indefinite expiration period in AWS CloudTrail, and you can customize this expiration period starting from one day and going up to 10 years.
- **Generate customized reporting of log data**: API call logs are used for analyzing user behavior and patterns by security experts and IT administrators. AWS CloudTrail produces log data with more than 25 fields to give you insights about system events for your AWS resources. You can use these fields to create comprehensive and customized reports for all users who accessed your resources by any medium. You can use log analysis tools for consuming near real-time log files generated by AWS CloudTrail and delivered to S3 buckets and other destinations of your choice. Moreover, AWS CloudTrail Logs events to enable and disable logging in AWS CloudTrail, thus allowing you to track whether the logging service is on or off.

AWS CloudTrail best practices

Let us look at best practices for AWS CloudTrail:

- Enable CloudTrail in all regions to track unused regions. It is a one-step configurable option that will ensure all activities are logged across all AWS regions.
- Enable log file validation; this is used to ensure integrity of a log file. These validated log files are invaluable during security audits and incident investigations.
- Always encrypt your logs at rest to avoid unauthorized usage of your log data.
- Always integrate AWS CloudTrail with CloudWatch Logs to configure metrics, alarms, searches, and notifications for your log data.
- Centralized logs from all your AWS accounts are used for a comprehensive and consolidated overview of your IT environment. Use the cross region replication feature of S3 to store all logs in one central location.

- Enable server access logging for S3 buckets that are storing CloudTrail log files to ensure all unauthorized access attempts are identified.
- Enforce MFA for deleting S3 buckets storing CloudTrail log data.
- Use IAM to restrict access to S3 buckets storing CloudTrail Logs. Also ensure write-only access for AWS CloudTrail is restricted to designated users.

Auditing in AWS

AWS engages with third party auditors and external certifying agencies to ensure all the controls, processes, and systems are in place for continuous compliance with various programs, certifications, compliance, standards, reports, and third party attestations.

Responsibility for auditing all controls and layers above physical resources in AWS lies with the customer, as we learnt while going through AWS shared security responsibility model. AWS provides all certifications and reports for reviews to the auditors.

AWS provides a customer compliance center to enable its customers to achieve greater security and compliance in the cloud. This center provides multiple resources such as case studies and white papers to learn ways to achieve compliance from AWS customers in highly regulated industries. It has a comprehensive set of resources and documentation to get your cloud governance plan in action. Visit `https://aws.amazon.com/compliance/customer-center/` to find out more about the customer compliance center at AWS.

AWS has an auditor learning path, designed for users in auditor, compliance, and legal roles. It teaches skills to audit all solutions deployed on the AWS cloud. AWS has case studies, white papers, auditing guides, checklists, audit guidelines and various self paced, virtual classroom and instructor led training in place to learn about auditing your resources, solutions, and IT environment in AWS cloud to ensure compliance. Visit `https://aws.amazon.com/compliance/auditor-learning-path/` to find out about the AWS auditor learning path.

In this section, we are going to learn about AWS services that help us with auditing in various capacities, such as auditing resource configuration through AWS Config or auditing security best practices through AWS Trusted Advisor. We will look through the AWS Service Catalog to ensure compliance by allowing pre-defined resources to be provisioned in our AWS environment. We will begin by learning about AWS Artifact, a fully managed self-service portal for accessing and downloading all industry certificates and compliance documents for your AWS resources that are required by your internal and external auditors.

AWS Artifact

AWS Artifact is an audit and compliance, self-service portal for accessing and downloading AWS Security and compliance reports and agreement without any additional charge. These reports include AWS **Service Organization Control (SOC)** reports, FedRAMP Partner Package, ISO 27001:2013, and so on from accreditation bodies across geographies and industry verticals that verify and validate AWS Security controls. AWS Artifact is accessible from the AWS Management Console.

You can use it for verifying and validating security control for any vertical in any geography. It helps you to identify the scope of each audit artifact, such as AWS service or resources, regions, and audit dates as well. AWS Artifact allows you to perform internal security assessments of your AWS resources. You can continuously monitor and assess the security of your AWS environment as audit reports are available as soon as new reports are released. There are agreements available in the AWS Artifact, such as the Business Associate Addendum and the **Non Disclosure Agreement (NDA)**.

The following image shows key AWS certifications and assurance programs. You can use AWS Artifact to download reports related to these certifications and programs along with many other programs and certifications:

Figure 16 - AWS certifications and assurance programs

AWS Config

AWS Config is a fully managed AWS service that helps you capture the configuration history for your AWS resources, maintain resource inventory, audit, and evaluate changes in resource configuration, and enables security and governance by integrating notifications with these changes. You can use it to discover AWS resources in your account, continuously monitor and evaluate resource configuration against desired resource configuration, export configuration details for your resource inventory, and find out the configuration details for a resource at given point in time.

A resource is any object that you create, update or delete in AWS, such as an EC2 instance, a S3 bucket, a security group, or an EBS volume. AWS Config is used to assess compliance as per internal guidelines for maintaining resource configurations. It enables compliance auditing, security analysis, resource change tracking, and operational troubleshooting. The following image shows the workflow for AWS Config, shown as follows:

1. A configuration change occurs for your AWS resource.
2. AWS Config records this change and normalizes it.
3. This change is delivered to a configurable S3 bucket.
4. Simultaneously, Config will evaluate this change against your desired configuration rules.
5. Config will display the result of configuration evaluation, it can send notifications of this evaluation as well if required.

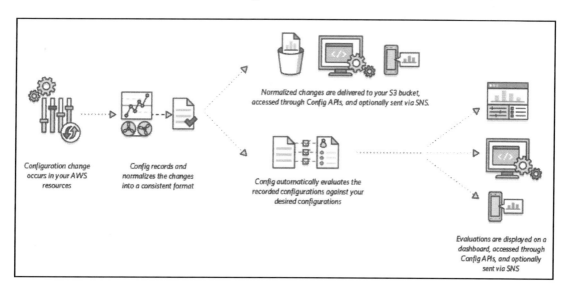

Figure 17 - AWS Config workflow

AWS Config use cases

- **Continuous audit and compliance**: AWS Config continuously validates and assesses the configuration of your resources against the configuration required as per your internal policies and compliance requirements. It also generates reports for your resource inventory and AWS infrastructure configurations for your auditors.

- **Compliance as code**: You can enable your system administrators to codify your best practices as Config rules for your resources to ensure compliance. These config rules can be custom rules created in AWS Lambda as per your compliance requirement. You can set up a rule as a periodic rule to run at configurable frequency or as a change triggered rule to run when a change is detected in resource configuration. AWS Config allows you to enforce self-governance among your users and automated assessments.

- **Security analysis**: Config rules can aid security experts in detecting anomalies arising out of a change in resource configuration. With the help of continuous assessment, security vulnerabilities can be detected in near real-time and the security posture of your environment can be examined. You can create 50 rules in your AWS account. This is a soft limit and can be increased by contacting the AWS Support.

The following figure shows a typical AWS Config dashboard. On the top left of the image, it shows **Total resource count** as **53** for this AWS account. There is **1 Noncompliant rule(s)** and there are **2 noncompliant resources(s)**. It also gives details about noncompliant rules, in this case it is **encrypted-volumes**:

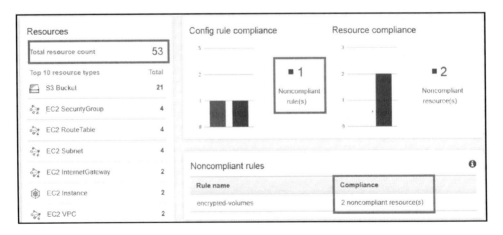

Figure 18 - AWS Config dashboard

AWS Trusted Advisor

AWS Trusted Advisor provides you with recommendations and real-time guidance on the following four areas to optimize your resources as per AWS best practices:

- Cost optimization
- Performance
- Security
- Fault tolerance

This service analyzes and checks your AWS environment in real-time on an ongoing basis. It integrates with AWS IAM so you can control access to checks as well as to categories. The status of these checks is displayed in the AWS Trusted Advisor dashboard under the following color coded scheme:

- Red: Action recommended
- Yellow: Investigation recommended
- Green: No problem detected

For all checks where the color is red or yellow, this service will provide alert criteria, recommended actions, and investigations along with resource details, such as details of the security groups that allow unrestricted access for specific ports.

By default, six core checks are available for all AWS customers, without any additional charges, to improve security and performance. These checks include five checks for security and one check for performance, that is, service limits, IAM use, security groups-unrestricted ports, MFA on root account, Elastic block storage public snapshot, and RDS public snapshot.

You can track any changes to status checks as most recent changes are placed at the top of the list in the AWS Trusted Advisor dashboard. You can refresh checks individually or refresh all at once. You can refresh a check once it is not refreshed for 5 minutes.

For other checks that are available with business or enterprise AWS support plans, you get the full benefits of AWS Trusted Advisor service. Apart from checks, you also get access to notifications with AWS weekly updates for your resource deployment. Alongside this, you also get programmatic access to AWS Trusted Advisor through the AWS Support API. This programmatic access allows you to retrieve and refresh AWS Trusted Advisor results.

AWS Service Catalog

AWS Service Catalog is a web service that enables organizations to enforce compliance by creating and managing pre-defined templates of AWS resources and services in the form of catalogs. These AWS resources and services can be EC2 instances, S3 buckets, EBS volumes, ELBs, databases, and so on that are required for running your applications in your IT environment. A Service Catalog will contain pre-approved resources for your users to provision and ensure a compliance and continuous governance across your AWS account.

AWS Service Catalog allows you to centrally manage your IT services in catalogs. You control availability, versions, and configuration of these IT services to people, departments, and cost centers in your organization to ensure compliance and adherence to corporate standards.

With a Service Catalog in place, your employees can go to project portfolios and quickly find and provision approved resources required to accomplish their task. When you update a product with a new version, your users are automatically notified of a new version update. Moreover, you can restrict resources geographically, such as allowing resources to be available only in certain AWS regions and allowable IP ranges as well.

This service integrates with AWS marketplace so you can add all products that you purchase from AWS Marketplace in the products catalog. You also have an option to tag your products. AWS Service Catalog provides you with a dashboard, products list, and provisioned products list in the AWS Management Console.

The following image depicts features available in the AWS Service Catalog. You can create and manage portfolios for your projects or assignments, add products such as AWS services or other resources in these portfolios along with all versions, configurations, and various constraints, and you can also manage user access to ensure how these products can be provisioned, who can use them, and where these products can be used:

Create and manage portfolios
Use portfolios to organize your products and distribute them to end users.

Add products
You can upload your line of business products or products you already own licenses to.

Manage user access
Decide who can access products and set policies on where and how users can launch them.

Figure 19 - AWS Service Catalog

AWS Security Audit Checklist

As an auditing best practice, ensure that security audits are performed periodically for your AWS account to meet compliance and regulatory requirements. To begin with, use AWS Trusted Advisor to audit security for your AWS account. Apart from periodic activity, an audit should be carried out in case of the following events:

- Changes in your organization
- One or more AWS services are no longer used
- If there is a change in the software or hardware configuration for your resources
- If there is a suspicious activity detected

The following is a list of AWS controls to be audited for security:

- Governance
- Network configuration and management
- Asset configuration and management
- Logical access control
- Data encryption
- Security logging and monitoring
- Security incident response
- Disaster recovery
- Inherited controls

Along with this checklist, there are various other guides to help you with auditing your AWS resources and AWS usage. Some of these guides are as follows and are available in the AWS auditor learning path at `https://aws.amazon.com/compliance/auditor-learning-path/`:

- AWS security audit guidelines
- Introduction to auditing the use of AWS
- Cybersecurity initiative audit guide

Summary

In this chapter, we went through the following core principles of a security solution in any IT environment, and understood how they are tightly coupled with each other:

- Logging
- Auditing
- Risk
- Compliance

We learnt about various services, tools, and features available in AWS to make our environment compliant and remain compliant. We looked at logging options available for major AWS services and how logging can be automated in multiple ways.

We learnt how we can use AWS CloudTrail along with S3 and CloudWatch Logs to automate storage, analysis, and notification of log files. We deep dived into best practices, features, use cases, and so on for AWS CloudTrail to understand logging at an extensive scale in AWS.

Furthermore, we looked into auditing in AWS, various services available for AWS users to enforce and ensure compliance, providing guardrails, and freedom to users to provision approved resources. We learnt about the AWS customer compliance center and AWS auditor learning path, dedicated resources for all those who work closely with audit and compliance.

In this section, we went over the following AWS services and learnt how each of them play a part in auditing, risks, and compliance in AWS:

- AWS Artifact
- AWS Config
- AWS Trusted Advisor
- AWS Service Catalog

Lastly, we learnt about auditing the security checklist and other guidelines and resources available for auditing usage in AWS.

In the next chapter, *AWS Security Best Practices*, we will learn about AWS security best practices. It will be a culmination of all that we have learnt so far in all the previous chapters regarding security in AWS. We will learn about solutions to ensure that best practices are met for all topics such as IAM, VPC, security of data, security of servers, and so on.

9

AWS Security Best Practices

Security at AWS is job zero. AWS is architected to be one of the most secure cloud environments with a host of built-in security features that allows it to eliminate most of the security overhead that is traditionally associated with IT infrastructure. Security is considered a shared responsibility between AWS and AWS customers where both of them work together to achieve their security objectives. We have looked at various services, tools, features, and third-party solutions provided by AWS to secure your assets on AWS. All customers share the following benefits of AWS security without any additional charges or resources:

- Keeping your data safe
- Meeting compliance requirements
- Saving money with in-built AWS security features
- Scaling quickly without compromising security

An enterprise running business-critical applications on AWS cannot afford to compromise on the security of these applications or the AWS environment where these applications are running. *As per Gartner, by 2020, 95% of all security breaches or incidents in cloud will be due to customer error and not from the cloud provider.*

Security is a core requirement for any **Information Security Management System (ISMS)** to prevent information from unauthorized access; theft, deletion, integrity compromise, and so on. A typical ISMS is not required to use AWS, however, AWS has a set of best practices lined up under the following topics to address widely adopted approaches for ensuring security for ISMS. You can use this approach if you have an ISMS in place:

- What shared security responsibility model is and how it works between AWS and customers
- Categorization and identifying your assets

- How to use privileged accounts and groups to control and manage user access to your data?
- Best practices for securing your data, network, servers, and operating systems
- How to achieve your security objectives using monitoring and alerting?

For more information on best practices on securing your ISMS, refer to the AWS Security Center at `https://aws.amazon.com/security/`. You can also use AWS Security Center for staying updated with the most common security issues and solutions to address these issues.

Security by design: There are the following two broad aspects of security in AWS:

- **Security of AWS environment**: AWS provides many services, tools, and features to secure your entire AWS environment including systems, networks, and resources such as encryption services, logging, configuration rules, identity management, and so on.
- **Security of hosts and applications**: Along with your AWS environment, you also need to secure applications that are running on AWS resources, data stored in the AWS resources, and operating systems on servers in AWS. This responsibility is primarily managed by AWS customers. AWS provides all tools and technologies available on-premises and used by the customer in AWS cloud as well.

Security by design is a four-phase systematic approach to ensure continuous security, compliance, and real-time auditing at scale. It is applicable for the security of AWS environment that allows for automation of security controls and streamlined audit processes. It allows customers to imbibe security and compliance reliably coded into AWS account. The following are four-phases of the Security by design approach:

- Understand your requirements
- Build a secure environment
- Enforce the use of templates
- Perform validation activities

Security in AWS is distributed at multiple layers such as AWS products and services, data security, application security, and so on. It is imperative to follow best practices for securing all such products and services to avoid getting your resources compromised in the AWS cloud.

Security is the number one priority for AWS and it is a shared responsibility between AWS and its customers. Security is imperative for all workloads deployed in the AWS environment. In AWS, storage is cheap, it should be used to store all logs and relevant records. It is recommended to use AWS managed services and in-built reporting services as much as possible for security to offload heavy lifting and enabling automation.

In this chapter, we will go over security best practices in AWS. These best practices are a combination of AWS recommendations, as well as expert advice and most common practices to follow in order to secure your AWS environment.

Our objective is to have a minimum security baseline for our workloads in the AWS environment by following these best practices that are spread across AWS services, products, and features. These security measures allow you to get visibility into the AWS usage and AWS resources and take corrective actions when required. They also allow automation at multiple levels, such as at the infrastructure level or at the application level to enable continuous monitoring and continuous compliance for all workloads deployed in AWS along with all AWS resources used in your AWS account.

We will learn about security best practices for the following topics:

- Shared security responsibility model
- IAM
- VPC
- Data security
- Security of servers
- Application security
- Monitoring, logging, and auditing

We will also look at **Cloud Adoption Framework (CAF)** that helps organizations embarking on their cloud journey with standards, best practices, and so on.

We will learn about the security perspective of CAF along with the following four components:

- Preventive
- Responsive
- Detective
- Directive

Shared security responsibility model

One of the first and most important requirements and security best practice to follow is to know about the AWS shared security responsibility model. Ensure that all stakeholders understand their share of security in AWS.

AWS is responsible for the security of cloud and underlying infrastructure that powers AWS cloud, and customers are responsible for security in the cloud, for anything they put in, and build on top of the AWS global infrastructure.

It is imperative to have clear guidelines about this shared security responsibility model in your organization. Identify resources that fall under your share of responsibilities, define activities that you need to perform, and publish a schedule of these activities to all stakeholders. The following figure shows the AWS shared security responsibility model:

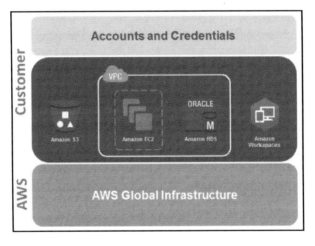

Figure 1 - AWS shared security responsibility model

IAM security best practices

IAM provides secure access control in your AWS environment to interact with AWS resources in a controlled manner:

- **Delete your root access keys**: A root account is one that has unrestricted access to all AWS resources in your account. It is recommended that you delete access keys, access key IDs, and the secret access key for the root account so that they cannot be misused. Instead, create a user with the desired permissions and carry on tasks with this user.

- **Enforce MFA**: Add an additional layer of security by enforcing MFA for all privileged users having access to critical or sensitive resources and APIs having a high blast radius.
- **Use roles instead of users**: Roles are managed by AWS; they are preferred over IAM users, as credentials for roles are managed by AWS. These credentials are rotated multiple times in a day and not stored locally on your AWS resource such as an EC2 instance.
- **Use access advisor periodically**: You should periodically verify that all users having access to your AWS account are using their access privileges as assigned. If you find that users are not using their privilege for a defined period by running the access advisor report, then you should revoke that privilege and remove the unused credentials. The following figure shows the security status as per AWS recommended IAM best practices in the AWS Management Console:

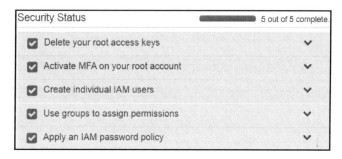

Figure 2 - AWS IAM security best practices

VPC

VPC is your own virtual, secured, scalable network in the AWS cloud that contains your AWS resources. Let us look at the VPC security best practices:

- **Create custom VPC**: It is recommended to create your own VPC and not use the default VPC as it has default settings to allow unrestricted inbound and outbound traffic.
- **Monitor VPC activity**: Create VPC flow logs to monitor flow of all IP traffic in your VPC from network resources to identify and restrict any unwanted activity.
- **Use Network Address Translation (NAT)**: Keep all your resources that do not need access to the internet in a private subnet. Use a NAT device, such as a NAT instance or NAT gateway to allow internet access to resources in a private subnet.

- **Control access**: Use IAM to control access to the VPC and resources that are part of the VPC. You can create a fine grained access control using IAM for resources in your VPC.
- **Use NACL**: Configure NACLs to define which traffic is allowed and denied for your VPC through the subnet. Control inbound and outbound traffic for your VPC. Use NACL to block traffic from specific IPs or range of IPs by blacklisting them.
- **Implement IDS/IPS**: Use AWS solutions for **Intrusion Detection System (IDS)** and **Intrusion Prevention System (IPS)** or reach out to AWS partners at the AWS marketplace to secure your VPC through one of these systems.
- **Isolate VPCs**: Create separate VPCs as per your use cases to reduce the blast radius in the event of an incident. For example, create separate VPCs for your development, testing, and production environments.
- **Secure VPC**: Utilize the web application firewall, firewall virtual appliance, and firewall solutions from the AWS marketplace to secure your VPC. Configure site to site VPN for securely transferring data between your on-premise data center and the AWS VPC. Use the VPC peering feature to enable communication between two VPCs in the same region. Place ELB in a public subnet and all other EC2 instances in a private subnet unless they need to access the internet by these instances.
- **Tier security groups**: Use different security groups for various tiers of your architecture. For example, have a security group for your web servers and have another one for database servers. Use security groups for allowing access instead of hard coded IP ranges while configuring security groups.

Data security

- **Encryption**: As a best practice to secure your data in AWS, *encrypt everything!* Encrypt your data at rest in AWS across your storage options. Automation and omnipresent, that's how you should design your encryption. Encrypting data helps you in the following ways:
  - Privacy
  - Integrity
  - Reliability
  - Anonymity

- **Use KMS**: Encryption using keys rely heavily on availability and security of keys. If you have the key, you have the data. Essentially, whoever owns the key, owns the data. So, ensure that you use a reliable and secure key management infrastructure for managing all your keys. AWS KMS is a fully managed service available for all your key management needs. Use this to manage your keys for encrypting data in S3, RDS, EBS volumes, and so on. Also, ensure that you control access to these keys through IAM permissions and policies.

- **Rotate your keys**: Ensure that keys are rotated periodically, usually quite frequently. The longer a key lives the higher is the security risk attached to it.

- **Classify your data**: Secure your data by classifying it, such as type of data, is it confidential information or is it publicly available? What would be the impact of loss or theft of this data? How sensitive is this data? What are the retention policies attached with this data? Moreover, classify data based on usage. Once you classify your data, you can choose the appropriate level of security controls and storage options in AWS for storing your data.

- **Secure data in transit**: Create a secure listener for your ELB to enable traffic encryption between clients initiating secure connection such as **Secure Socket Layer (SSL)** or **Transport Layer Security (TLS)** and your AWS ELB. This will help you secure your data in transit as well for applications running on EC2 instances. You can have similar configurations, known as TLS termination for other AWS services, such as Redshift, RDS, and all API endpoints. Use VPN, VPC Peering and Direct Connect to securely transfer data through VPC to other data sources.

- **S3 bucket permissions**: Ensure that you do not have world readable and world listable S3 buckets in your account. Restrict access to your buckets using IAM, access control lists, and bucket policies.

Security of servers

Let us look at best practices to secure your servers in AWS cloud:

- **Use IAM roles for EC2**: Always use IAM roles instead of IAM users for applications running on your EC2 instances. Assign a role to your EC2 instance for accessing other AWS services. This way, credentials for the role will not be stored in your EC2 instance like they are in case of an IAM user.

- **Use ELB**: Put all your EC2 instances behind AWS ELB when applicable. In this configuration, you will shield your instances from receiving traffic directly from the internet and they will receive traffic only from the AWS ELB.

- **Security group configuration**: A security group is a virtual firewall for your instance. It is imperative to configure it to secure your instances. Avoid allow all traffic, that is, opening up all ports for CIDR range of 0.0.0.0/0 in your security group. Instead, allow a limited range of IP addresses to access your EC2 instances. Similarly, for your web servers, allow traffic only on port 80 and port 443 for HTTP and HTTPS traffic.

- **Use Web Application Firewall (WAF)**: Use WAF and AWS shields to mitigate the risk of **Denial of Service (DoS)** or **Distributed Denial of Service (DDoS)** attacks. WAF lets you monitor traffic for your web application. It features deep packet inspection of all web traffic for your instances and allows you to take proactive action. You can set rules in WAF to blacklist IP addresses serving unwanted traffic to your web application.

- **Secured access**: Configure access for your servers using IAM. Use roles, federated access, or IAM users based on access requirements. Ensure that .pem files are password protected on all machines that need access to instances. Rotate credentials such as access keys that are required to access your instances. Use **Secure Token Service (STS)** for granting temporary credentials instead of using IAM user credentials.

- **Backup and recovery**: Use snapshots to back up all data and configuration stored on your servers. Create **Amazon Machine Image (AMI)** for your instance to use in the event of a disaster to recover your instance. Ensure that you are regularly testing the backup and recovery process for your servers.

- **EC2 termination protection**: Always enable termination protection for your mission-critical EC2 instances so your instances do not get accidentally deleted through an API request or through the AWS Management Console.

Application security

Let us look at best practices to secure applications developed and deployed in AWS servers and other AWS resources:

- **Use web application firewall**: Always use WAF to detect and filter unwanted HTTP and HTTPS traffic for your web application. Automate WAF rules to block such traffic by integrating with AWS Lambda. Implement DevOps culture in your organization, ensuring that securing is not just responsibility of operations, instead, security should be built-in inside applications.

- **Amazon Inspector**: Use an agent-based security assessment, such as an AWS Inspector for your web applications and for servers that are used to run these web applications. It has built-in rule packages to identify common vulnerabilities for various standards and benchmarks. You can automate security responses by configuring APIs of Amazon Inspector. You should regularly run these assessments to ensure there isn't any security threat as per the existing configuration for your web application and servers.

- **Penetration testing**: AWS allows you to conduct vulnerability and penetration testing for all your EC2 instances. You need to request the AWS console and AWS support to conduct these tests in advance before you actually conduct them.

- **Utilize AWS security tools**: AWS provides several tools for encryption and key management such as KMS and cloud hardware security module, firewalls such as web application firewall, AWS shield, security groups, and NACLs, and so on. Integrate your application with these tools to provide greater security and threat protection.

Monitoring, logging, and auditing

Let us look at best practices for monitoring, logging, and auditing in AWS:

- **Log everything**: AWS provides AWS CloudTrail that logs all API activities for your AWS account. Enable this service for all regions and create a trail to audit these activities whenever required. Take advantage of the AWS cloud-native logging capabilities for all AWS services. Collect, store, and process logs for infrastructure such as VPC flow logs, AWS services, and logs for your applications to ensure continuous monitoring and continuous compliance. Use CloudWatch Logs to process all log data, and S3 for storing it.

- **Enable AWS CloudWatch**: Ensure that you are using AWS CloudWatch to monitor all your resources in AWS including data, services, servers, applications, and other AWS native tools and features such as ELBs, auto scaling groups, and so on. Use metrics, dashboards, graphs, and alarms to create preventive solutions for security incidents.

- **Continuous compliance**: Use AWS Trusted Advisor to proactively check for issues related to security configuration of your AWS resources. Set up a pre-defined inventory for all your hardware and software resources including versions and configurations in the AWS service catalog to provide a guardrail for your users, helping them to choose only compliant resources for their workloads. Use AWS Config to notify the user in real time about changes in configuration from their pre-defined configuration of resources.

- **Automate compliance and auditing**: Use combinations of AWS CloudTrail, AWS SNS, AWS Lambda, AWS Config Rules, CloudWatch Logs, CloudWatch Alerts, Amazon Inspector, and so on to automate compliance and auditing for all resources and all workloads deployed in your AWS account.

AWS CAF

AWS CAF helps organizations migrating to cloud computing in their cloud adoption journey by providing best practices and guidance through this framework. It breaks down this guidance into manageable areas of focus for building cloud-based systems that can be mapped to individual units of organizations. These focus areas are known as **perspectives**, there are six of these. Each perspective is further broken into components.

There are three perspectives, each for business (business, people, and governance) and technology (platform, security, and operations) stakeholders as shown in the following figure:

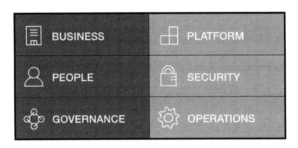

Figure 3 - AWS Cloud Adoption Framework perspectives

Each perspective is made up of responsibilities owned by one or more stakeholders known as CAF capabilities. These capabilities are standards, skills, and processes that define what is owned and/or managed by these stakeholders for their organizations cloud adoption journey. You would map these capabilities with roles within your organizations and identify gaps in your existing stakeholder, standards, skills, and processing towards your cloud journey.

Security perspective

The security perspective provides guidance for aligning organizational requirements relating to security control, resilience, and compliance for all workloads developed and deployed in AWS cloud. It lists out processes and skills required for stakeholders to ensure and manage security in cloud. It helps you select security controls and structure them as per your organization's requirements to transform the security culture in your organization.

The security perspective has capabilities that target the following roles in an organization: Chief Information Security Officer, IT Security Managers, IT Security Analysts, Head of Audit and Compliance, and all resources in Auditing and Compliance roles.

The security perspective consists of the following four components:

Directive component

This component provides guidance to all stakeholders that are either operating or implementing a security controls in your environment on planning your security approach for migrating to the AWS cloud. It includes controls, such as security operations playbook and runbooks, least privilege access, data locality, change and asset management, and so on. The directive component includes activities such as monitoring the teams through centralized phone and email distribution lists, integrating development, security, and operations teams roles and responsibilities to create a culture of DevSecOps in your organizations.

Preventive component

This component is responsible for providing guidance for implementing a security infrastructure within your organization and with AWS. You should enable your security teams to build skills such as automation, deployment for securing your workloads in agile, dynamic, elastic, and scalable cloud environments. This component builds on identification of security controls as identified in the directive component. In this component, you learn to work with these controls, for example, you will look at your data protection policies and procedures and tweak them if required. Similarly, you will revisit your identity and access measures and infrastructure protection measures too. Consider establishing a minimum security baseline as part of this component.

Detective component

This component deals with logging and monitoring to help you gain visibility into the security posture of your organization. Logging and monitoring along with events analysis, testing will give you operational agility as well as transparency for security controls you have defined and operate regularly. This component includes activities such as security testing, asset inventory, monitoring and logging, and change detection. You should consider defining your logging requirements keeping AWS native logging capabilities in mind alongside conducting vulnerability scans and penetration testing as per AWS pre-defined process.

Responsive component

This chapter guides you to respond to any security events for your organization by incorporating your existing security policies with AWS environment. It guides you to automate your incident response and recovery processes thereby enabling you to provide more resources toward performing forensics and root cause analysis activities for these incidents. It includes activities such as forensics, incident response, and security incident response simulations. You should consider updating and automating your school responses as per the AWS environment and validating them by running simulations.

Summary

In this chapter, we went over security best practices for all the topics we have covered in all previous chapters, such as IAM, VPC, security of data, security of servers, and so on. Throughout this chapter, we have focused on and emphasized on security automation by utilizing AWS native services, tools, and features. AWS security best practices echo similar recommendations as well to create a software-defined, self-healing environment by using AWS-managed services instead of building something manually.

We also learnt about AWS CAF, that is used by hundreds of organizations to help them migrate to cloud in their cloud journey. We deep dived into the security perspective of this framework and learnt about four components of security perspective that will help us secure our workloads while migrating to the AWS cloud.

Index

Printed in Great Britain
by Amazon